T0139255

EFFECTIVE
USE of TEAMS
FOR
IT AUDITS

EFFECTIVE USE OF TEAMS FOR IT AUDITS

MARTIN A. KRIST

AUERBACH

Boca Raton   London   New York   Washington, D.C.

Library of Congress Cataloging-in-Publication Data

Effective Use of Teams for IT Audits / Martin A. Krist, editor.
      p. cm.
    Includes bibliographical references.
    ISBN 0-8493-9828-2 (alk. paper)
    1. Electronic data processing--Auditing Standards. I. Krist,
Martin A.
QA76.9.A93S73   1999
658.4'78--dc21   99-31313
                                                              CIP

This book contains information obtained from authentic and highly regarded sources. Reprinted material is quoted with permission, and sources are indicated. A wide variety of references are listed. Reasonable efforts have been made to publish reliable data and information, but the author and the publisher cannot assume responsibility for the validity of all materials or for the consequences of their use.

Neither this book nor any part may be reproduced or transmitted in any form or by any means, electronic or mechanical, including photocopying, microfilming, and recording, or by any information storage retrieval system, without prior permission in writing from the publisher.

All rights reserved. Authorization to photocopy items for internal or personal use, or the personal or internal use of clients, may be granted by CRC Press LLC, provided that $.50 per page photocopied is paid directly to Copyright Clearance Center, 222 Rosewood Drive, Danvers, MA 01923 USA. The fee code for users of the Transactional Reporting Service is ISBN 0-8493-9828-2/99/$0.00 + $.50. The fee is subject to change without notice. For organizations that have been granted a photocopy license by the CCC, a separate system of payment has been arranged.

The consent of CRC Press LLC does not extend to copying for general distribution, for promotion, for creating new works, or for resale. Specific permission must be obtained in writing from CRC Press LLC for such copying.

Direct all inquiries to CRC Press LLC, 2000 Corporate Blvd., N.W., Boca Raton, Florida, 33431.

Trademark Notice: Product or corporate names may be trademarks or registered trademarks, and are used only for identification and explanation, without intent to infringe.

© 2000 by CRC Press LLC

Auerbach is an imprint of CRC Press LLC

No claim to original U.S. Government works

International Standard Book Number 0-8493-9828-2

Printed in the United State of America 1 2 3 4 5 6 7 8 9 0

Printed on acid-free paper

Contents

WORKPAPERS

Contents

Introduction

Most organizations find that an empowered team will improve the effectiveness of an IT audit. Such a team has the appropriate authority, resources, and skills to perform a project, determine the solution, and implement that solution without outside intervention. Audit management should establish certain guidelines for teams to follow. Management may approve team assignments, but the team can use whatever resources necessary to complete that assignment.

This supplement suggests four approaches to ensure the effective use of teams:

1. Assessing team effectiveness. An auditing function can use a self-assessment document to determine whether it uses teams effectively.
2. Organizing and managing teams. Several suggestions are provided for staffing, organizing, and managing these teams.
3. Using teams to conduct reviews during an audit. This six-step approach uses peers to review peers, as opposed to supervisors to control subordinates. The review process provides checklists for use when conducting these peer reviews.
4. Using teams to improve audit processes. A detailed six-step improvement process is provided as a tool for improving audit processes.

Team tools are significant to ultimate team success. This supplement includes suggestions for building a team toolbox and an appendix that describes effective team tools.

Chapter 1
Self Assessing Team Effectiveness

A traditional team is a group of people working together on a project. It includes a team leader (in an audit, that person is usually a senior auditor) and operates under management constraints. This supplement uses the word *team* to describe empowered teams, defined as a group of people working together on a project who have the necessary authority, resources, and skills to perform that project without intervention from management. Empowered does not mean full authority to do anything. Once given a project to complete or an area of responsibility, the team decides what needs to be done and does it without obtaining additional management consent.

ASSESSING THE EFFECTIVENESS OF TEAMS IN AN ORGANIZATION

Many managers believe they have already embraced the team concept when their the teams are not effective. Their misperception is normally associated with their concept of what a team is and how it operates. Most people perceive that a team is a group of people under the direction of a team manager or leader. The team is usually only as good as the team manager because the manager directs and controls its efforts. In some instances, even the team manager cannot make decisions but must present plans and results to higher levels of management for approval.

The self-assessment checklist in Workpaper 1-1 is designed to help auditors evaluate how effectively teams perform in their organizations. This test can be performed by an individual or by a group of individuals using a consensus tool to develop a yes or no response. As a general rule, the use of a group is far superior to having an individual complete the self-assessment.

The self-assessment should be completed next, before reading any further.

EVALUATING THE RESULTS OF THE SELF-ASSESSMENT

This self-assessment tests to see whether an organization uses common practices associated with effective teams. The auditor should total the number of "yes" responses in the evaluation. "Not applicable" responses should be considered "yes" responses, but if an auditor has more than two "not applicable" responses, the assessment guide found in Exhibit 1-1 is probably not valid.

Exhibit 1-1. Self-Assessment Test Evaluation

Number of Yes Responses	Evaluation
13–15	You use empowered teams effectively. Use the materials in this manual to fine-tune your approach.
10–12	Your audit organization has empowered teams in place, but there are opportunities for improvement. Use the materials in this manual to improve your use of teams.
7–9	Your audit organization has implemented some important team concepts, but the teams do not have the necessary authority or resources to be effective. Team results probably vary from very successful to near failure. Current team members and managers should discuss this self-assessment to identify areas of conflict and then use the manual to identify solutions.
4–6	Most likely, your teams have some of the attributes of empowered teams, but management probably retains control adequate to stop the teams from taking action that is unacceptable to audit management. Audit management needs to decide if it wants empowered teams, and if it does, it must delegate the authority and resources necessary to make the teams effective. Management may wish to do this in a pilot effort so that it can see that empowered teams work.
0–3	Your audit organization does not believe in empowered teams. This audit manual explains what empowered teams are and how they operate. It can help your organization decide whether empowered teams should be introduced into your audit function.

Workpaper 1-1. Audit Team Effectiveness Self-Assessment

	Response			
Item	**Yes**	**No**	**N/A**	**Comments**
1. Does audit management believe that team members can and should make the majority of decisions that affect how they do their work?				
2. Does audit management believe that team members can suggest and implement improvements to their work without going through several levels of approval?				
3. Does management believe that much of the work in audit lends itself to a team-based approach rather than to an individual effort?				
4. Does the physical design of your audit workplace lend itself to working in teams?				
5. Is it possible to organize audit work and audit process improvement efforts so that teams of auditors can take responsibility for entire jobs?				
6. Is the audit staff willing to take the initiative and authority needed to make teams work?				
7. Does the overall audit organizational culture, vision, and values support teamwork and empowerment?				
8. Is there a history in your audit function of empowering teams to develop their own plans and solutions and implement them without management approval?				
9. Are audit managers willing to adjust their responsibilities downward and radically change their role and behavior?				
10. Is audit employment secure enough to guarantee a period of relative stability during which teams can develop?				
11. Is your auditing function willing to support team activities by providing them with adequate support resources, such as clerical support, and by providing teams with information, coaching, and training?				
12. Is audit management willing to invest in the resources and time necessary to develop teams into effective groups?				

Workpaper 1-1. Audit Team Effectiveness Self-Assessment (Continued)

Item	Response			Comments
	Yes	No	N/A	
13. Does your audit function have the systems necessary to provide teams timely information to support their team activities?				
14. Does the audit staff have the necessary team skills to be effective operating as team members?				
15. Is audit management willing to permit teams to operate without appointing a manager/leader for the team?				

Chapter 2
Using Teams Versus Taking a Hierarchical Approach

Empowered teams function effectively only in a Total Quality Management (TQM) culture. TQM is a management philosophy based on ideas proposed for decades by such quality leaders as Dr. W. Edwards Deming, Dr. Joseph Juran, and Stephen Covey. TQM consists of continuous process improvement activities that involve everyone in an organization. The use of teams is an integral component of TQM.

Central to the TQM approach is a change in management philosophy regarding responsibility and authority. Before, authority rested with management, who directed the work of subordinates. Today, the responsibility for quality work rests with everyone, from top management to the lowest position in the organization.

TQM uses a team organization where both management and employees are members of teams. Those who do a job know it best; therefore, in TQM suggestions to improve the quality of a particular process come from the employees who work in the process and the managers who work on the process. Communication is encouraged to promote employees and management who work together to continuously improve processes.

A culture encompasses management philosophy, organizational values, and employee attitudes. It directly reflects an organization's managerial infrastructure. A TQM culture incorporates the tenets of TQM management by process, continuous improvement, partnership, empowerment, teamwork, and training.

BUILDING A TQM CULTURE

Building a TQM culture involves changing an organization's existing culture. The management philosophies that dominate North American corporations today increasingly reflect TQM principles. Upper management establishes the strategic directions and then works to support technical implementation of that strategy by the use of the organization.

Middle management, once a significant obstacle to the TQM approach, has largely been eliminated over the past decade. These managers fell victim to the right-sizing and down-sizing effort over that time.

Nonmanagement personnel work to achieve the organization's strategic objectives. They have increasing latitude to make decisions and often have the authority to spend within certain limits. The good of the organization necessarily comes first.

Many organizations have not embraced TQM despite the many that have embraced it. To contrast the TQM culture with the past, consider the following description of the classical hierarchical organization.

TQM Infrastructure

In a TQM-driven organization, upper management establishes an inspiring vision for the organization. It leads the movement toward that vision by organizing and influencing staff. It lives the vision. The vision inspires, enables, challenges, encourages risk, and dares employees to be great. The vision becomes the mission of the organization.

Middle management facilitates, advises, and teaches the remaining organization. It partners with the staff to develop objectives that address the organizational mission and empowers them to develop and execute supporting tactical plans. It is continuously involved in the effort to improve the organization's work processes and support the strategic vision.

The staff, supported by middle management, work as self-managing teams. They develop and execute tactical plans and projects that support the information technology (IT) mission. The established self-managing teams are building blocks for improving quality throughout the organization.

It has been difficult building a TQM culture. It involved reversing the established management norm from the last 100 years.

The building process can begin with small incremental changes in the way business is conducted:

- Making a phone call or office visit instead of writing a memo or sending an e-mail.
- Identifying and praising people for working as a team instead of individually.
- Identifying and praising people for working with other functional areas.
- Implementing training in communication, facilitation, and problem solving.

This building process is not strictly a tactical activity. The strategy is also important for effecting change and demonstrating success in the short term. It should include approaches that can be incorporated into daily, weekly, or monthly work schedules without disrupting current responsibilities. If TQM integration interferes with achieving short-term objectives, obstructing the effort the TQM effort is likely to fail.

DIFFERENCES BETWEEN TRADITIONAL AND EMPOWERED TEAM ORGANIZATIONS

Exhibit 2-1 details how teams perform in a traditional hierarchical organization and in a TQM culture. A more detailed description is provided in the following sections.

Exhibit 2-1. Team Performance in Organizations with Hierarchical and TQM Cultures

Team Characteristic	Hierarchical Organization	TQM Culture
Job assignment	Narrow—normally a single task	Involves whole processes
Organizational structure	Headed by an appointed team manager	Characterized by consensus management
Information flow	Limited and controlled	Open and shared
Audit management's role	Approves recommendations	Coaches
Use of tools	Limited	Extensive
Use of processes	Limited	Extensive
Rewards	Part of an individual's job	Team-based
Training	Of minimal importance (supervisor will direct individuals)	Requires training in team skills and tools

Job assignment

In a hierarchical organization, a team is usually organized to solve a single task (e.g., to evaluate a specific audit tool). In a TQM culture, teams operate continually on work processes, deciding when to focus on specific tasks. For example, the team working on improving the audit process may choose to consider audit software. The members would consider how that tool would be integrated into the total audit process.

Organizational structure

In a hierarchical organization, teams tend to be hierarchical. In a TQM culture, all team members are equal. They elect their own leader and usually operate by consensus.

Information flow

Hierarchical organizations tend to control the flow of information throughout the organization, and information normally flows downward. In a TQM culture, there is open and free access to information. The team has whatever information it needs to do its work, or the authenticity to get it, without obtaining specific management permission to access that information.

Management's role

In a hierarchical structure, management normally receives recommendations, evaluates them, and decides whether to approve them. In a TQM culture, the team can, within limits, approve its own recommendations and implement those recommendations without peer approval. Management facilitates team efforts.

Use of tools

In a hierarchical structure, management decides what tools a team needs. In a TQM culture, the staff decides. Management knows they will develop effective solutions because teams in TQM cultures have well-defined processes and tools.

Use of processes

In a hierarchical structure, the team manager directs the team workers. Results are usually more important than processes, and performance is evaluated on an individual basis. In a TQM culture, management accepts ultimate responsibility for results, and teams are held accountable for following processes.

Rewards

In a hierarchical structure, teams are part of individual performance. People tend to be evaluated by their supervisors on their individual performance. In a TQM culture, teams are rewarded on team performance. Teams may even have the authority to allocate rewards within the team although that should only be exercised in exceptional situations.

Training

In a hierarchical structure, training is frequently viewed as a reward, not a necessary component of job performance. Individuals can be supervised and directed to lessen the importance of training, and personnel are assumed to have acquired needed skills elsewhere. In a TQM environment, the ability to follow processes and use tools is a necessary condition. Training is just another tool.

MOVING FROM TEAMS IN A HIERARCHICAL ORGANIZATION TO TEAMS IN A TQM CULTURE

No function can move from hierarchical organization to a TQM culture overnight. Likewise, an IT audit function with teams operating in a hierarchical organization cannot be restructured to empower these teams overnight. Two things can be done to support this change. First, the audit teams must begin to structure themselves and operate as teams in a TQM culture. Job assignments for teams must be expanded in scope. An action plan can be developed to change team structure and performance. Establish the eight TQM team characteristics as goals. Develop plans to move toward these characteristics.

Second, the audit function should strive to score 15 yes answers on the team effectiveness self-assessment checklist. For each negative answer, an action plan should be developed to change the function's culture. The organization may wish to begin with one or two items that would be easiest to implement in its culture.

This supplement proposes two ways for teams to improve the IT audit process. First, review audit results, and second, improve the audit process.

Chapter 3
Using Teams for Reviewing IT Audits

There are four major objectives of an information technology (IT) audit review:

- *Emphasize quality throughout the audit process.* All IT audit projects have four factors that must be continuously monitored and adjusted for control to be maintained over the development process. They are scope, schedule, resources, and quality. The factors can be viewed as dials on a control panel. When one dial is adjusted, one or more of the others must be adjusted to compensate. Reviews can be performed throughout the audit process, ensuring that the quality factor receives the same priority as the others.
- *Detect defects when and where they are introduced (where they are cheapest to correct).* Studies show that in most installations more defects originate in the planning process than in the audit process. In other words, most defects are introduced early in the audit. Total Quality Management (TQM), unlike traditional audit control techniques (i.e., the review of working papers by supervisors), can be conducted during these crucial early stages. Finding and correcting defects soon after they are inserted not only prevents cascading mistakes later in the audit but also provides important clues regarding their root causes.
- *Provide a logical opportunity to involve auditors in the audit process.* IT auditor involvement during the audit process is essential. An auditor's traditional role has been to supply information for the audit. Reviews give auditors another opportunity to confirm that IT audit data and findings are current.
- *Permit midcourse corrections.* Reviews are consistent with audit approaches that recognize the need for change. They highlight the need for change. Because reviews are performed throughout the audit, they support these approaches by adding the auditor perspective throughout the audit and stopping unwanted or wrong audit tasks from being performed.

RISK ANALYSIS

A plan should be developed for each major audit effort or project. A risk assessment should be performed before preparing the plan. It should do the following:

- Determine the audit's importance to the company.
- Assess the audit's probability of success.
- Identify potential problem areas.
- Identify or select quality factors to be used during the review.

Workpaper 3-1 can be used to document the information gathered during risk analysis.

USING REVIEWS

High risk audits require more effort to review. Reviews can be used to reduce the following types of risks:

Risk	Action
Vague audit requirements	Perform reviews early in audit cycle to ensure that audit requirements are specific.
Ineffective use of audit tools or techniques.	Review products affected by those tools or techniques.
Critical performance, security, or control requirements.	Review audit plans.
No margin for error.	Perform reviews throughout the audit cycle.

Once an IT auditor decides to perform reviews, he or she should include review tasks in the audit plan. Reviews should be activities within the scope of the audit, not concurrent or external. The reviews should be scheduled and resources allocated as with any other audit activity.

REVIEW PREREQUISITES

The prerequisites for a successful review program are as follows:

- *An audit process.* Reviews are documentation reviews and should be done in a standard framework. The more well-defined the products, the more options available.
- *Management support.* Techniques to get such support for reviews include the following:

    —Learning review economics.
    —Enlisting auditees support. It is important to explain to auditees the economic and schedule advantages that reviews provide and to solicit their support for the process.

Workpaper 3-1. Audit Risk Analysis

Audit Risk	Magnitude			Analysis and Action
	High	Medium	Low	

—Performing pilot-type reviews and evaluating their impact.
—Bringing in outside experts to sell the idea.

- *Reviewing process.* It is necessary to develop a process for these reviews.
- *Staff support.* Effective techniques include the following:

  —Conducting pilot projects to demonstrate the benefits of reviews.
  —Demonstrating management support.
  —Reducing the hassle by supplying consulting and administrative support.
  —Using the results of reviews constructively. Staff members should not be evaluated on the quality or number of defects in their products during reviews. The following questions should be part of the staff evaluation process: Does the employee willingly participate adequately prepare. Does the employee follow the process (i.e., complete assignments on time and show up for meetings)?
  —Scheduling adequate time for reviews.
  —Making the reviews a win-win situation. The project leader and staff should be thanked for conducting the review, regardless of whether it works.
  —Finding a reward to give all participants during any review trial period, such as public recognition, a plaque, or a group dinner.

- *Training.* People cannot conduct effective reviews unless they are trained. It is necessary to provide training in initial concepts and skills, as well as offer follow-up training.

THE CHECKPOINT PROCESS

Checkpoint reviews occur at predefined points in an audit to evaluate its effectiveness. These reviews test whether the audit is adequately addressing critical quality factors.

The checkpoint review process consists of two phases. The first is a planning phase that occurs at the beginning of each project targeted for checkpoint reviews. The second phase includes the steps for conducting a checkpoint review. Repeat this phase for each checkpoint review held during the project. These phases are summarized in Exhibit 3-1.

PHASE ONE: PLANNING

The planning phase contains two steps, establishing review objectives and developing the review plan.

Phase One: Planning

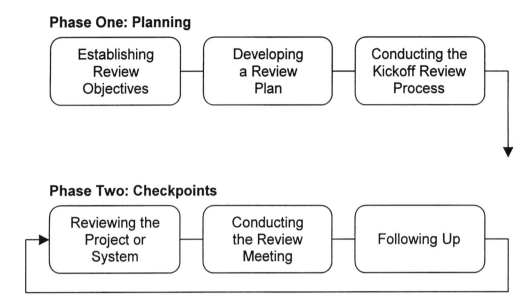

Phase Two: Checkpoints

Exhibit 3-1. The Checkpoint Review Process

Step One: Establishing Review Objectives

The objective of this step is to identify and confirm the vital quality factors for the system being reviewed. The review administrator performs this task before the project starts.

Task One: Selecting the Review Chairperson. A review chairperson must be selected to coordinate and oversee the checkpoint review process. This person may be an end user, professional facilitator, development team member, or independent group. The chairperson must do the following:

- Select quality factors.
- Set the review schedule.
- Make review assignments.
- Determine review procedures.
- Select review checklists.
- Train reviewers.
- Administer the review process.
- Run review meetings.
- Participate as a reviewer (this is optional).
- Write final review reports.

The chairperson is responsible for the success of the review and (in part) the success of the project. He or she must be a member of the senior staff, possess management skills, be respected, and communicate effectively. A communicator is preferable to a technician. He or she must be able to allocate the time required to do the job properly. It is often advisable to use an independent person. The chairperson will interact with a team best if he or she does the following:

- Teaches the team how to give and take criticism.
- Builds enthusiasm for finding errors.
- Starts and stops review meetings on time.
- Limits the length of any one meeting.
- Avoids reviewing too much material at one meeting.
- Does not surprise the review team with new review criteria or new review rules.
- Does not discuss material the review team does not have.
- Understands how much time is required for review preparation.
- Considers team seating arrangements.
- Invites experts to critique the review process.

Task Two: Identifying Quality Factors. This step determines the critical quality factors (i.e., desired results from system) that will focus the review efforts for this particular project. Quality factors are categories of system attributes. They enable customers and producers to describe those attributes with a common vocabulary. In addition, the factors that are ranked most important affect the system architecture, assuming that there are inadequate time and budget constraints to satisfy all factors. For example, a system that needs data accuracy requires many controls, whereas a system that needs maintainability might need resources spent on documentation and system simplicity.

In the checkpoint review process, ten quality factors should be organized into three groups: data issues, operational issues, and program issues.

- *Data issues.* Data issues affect the quality of information entered into, processed, stored, and reported to the IT auditor. There are four quality factors in this group:

    1. *Accuracy and completeness.* Structure and controls governing data entry; data storage and the accuracy and completeness of information.
    2. *Authorization.* Controls to determine that information is processed in accordance with the policies and intent of management.
    3. *Workpaper integrity.* The custodial responsibility of auditor information.
    4. *Reconstruction.* Retention of logs and other means that permit information users to determine how data was authorized, entered, and processed. This quality factor answers the question, "How did this type of auditing occur?"

- *Operational issues.* Operational issues are quality factors relating to the performance of the audit effort. This group contains four quality factors:

  5. *Continuity of processing.* The ability to retain the integrity of the audit process so that IT auditing can continue if personnel change.
  6. *Service levels.* The speed at which processing can occur while maintaining required effectiveness.
  7. *Security.* The protection of resources against unauthorized modification, destruction, misuse, and disclosure.
  8. *Cost-effectiveness.* The economics of auditing.

- *Program issues.* Program issues are the implemented functionality and structure of the end-user or customer needs. This group includes two quality factors:

  9. *Audit objectives.* Meeting the true needs of the organization.
  10. *Compliance.* Ensuring that the audit meets the standards of government, industry, and organizations.

These quality factors can be customized by doing the following:

- Changing the name of a quality factor to a term more appropriate for the organization.
- Adding additional quality factors to cover topics that were overlooked.
- Consolidating two or more factors into one category.
- Adding a business factor that may take on great importance during the audit.

Quality factors should be ranked on Workpaper 3-2. The criteria for ranking critical quality factors are as follows:

- The customer's perspective of what is important.
- Application functional requirements.
- Project risks.
- Project constraints.
- Common causes of failures.
- IT management concerns.

The application and project characteristics will already have been examined during risk analysis. They should form the basis for selecting the quality factors.

Emphasis on one quality factor can make it impossible to satisfy another factor. For example, cost-effectiveness may be critical because of a tight schedule or budget constraints, but concentrating on cost-effectiveness might make it impossible to meet all audit objectives.

Workpaper 3-2. Quality Factor Ranking

Quality Factor	Rank	Comments
Accuracy or Completeness		
Authorization		
Workpaper Integrity		
Reconstruction		
Continuity of Processing		
Service Level		
Security		
Cost-Effectiveness		
Audit Objectives		
Compliance		

Task Three: Confirming the Review Process and Objectives. This step describes the review process and confirms quality factors with IT, customers, and project management. The chairperson of the review team should confirm the following consensus items before initiating reviews:

- The value of review.
- That quality factors are properly ranked.
- That adequate time will be allocated for reviews.
- That reviewers will be released from other tasks to perform the review.
- Who will get the review reports.

Workpaper 3-3 is a work program for confirming the review concept. If the chairperson finds that any of the items in this workpaper are not supported, he should address these roadblocks early in the review process. Even if he or she cannot get true support, the chairperson may be able to reduce active opposition to the review concept and convert people to a wait-and-see-if-it-works attitude.

Step Two: Developing a Review Plan

The objective of this step is to select and train reviewers, conduct a background review, and develop a detailed work plan. The reviewers perform this step before project initiation.

Task One: Establishing a Review Team. Experts must be selected based on the project's quality factors. Training must be provided if necessary. Potential candidates include auditee personnel, other auditors, IT audit specialists, and outside consultants (e.g., vendors, security experts). The reviewer must do the following:

- Review the audit at predefined checkpoints.
- Assess the audit in terms of predefined quality concerns.
- Document findings and issues.
- Make recommendations to the audit team.

The reviewer is responsible for the success of the review and, in part, the success of the project. He or she must know the quality factor area; be respected, fair, and objective; have time available; and believe in the review concept.

Reviewer candidates include individuals who have previously performed reviews effectively, respected auditee staff, specialists in quality factors, etc. Recruit candidates by meeting with him or her and explaining why that person is needed. It is important to explain the necessary commitment in time and responsibility and to identify training that will be given. Emphasize the importance of the project being successful. Tips for getting good reviewers include the following:

Workpaper 3-3. Review Confirmation Checklist

Item	Yes	No	N/A	Comments
1. Does senior management support the review concept?				
2. Does the audit project team support the review concept?				
3. Does the auditor support the review concept?				
4. Does the auditor agree with the quality factor ranking?				
5. Does the audit team understand and agree with the quality factor ranking?				
6. Has time been included in the audit project schedule for reviews?				
7. Do the involved audit supervisors support releasing their staff to participate in reviews of other audit projects?				
8. Do all involved parties understand and agree who will get copies of the review reports?				

- Limiting their involvement.
- Making assignments specific.
- Providing adequate training.
- Getting their managers' support first.

Workpaper 3-4 can be used to match reviewers with areas to be reviewed.

Reviewers must be trained in audit methodology, review objectives and process, and interpersonal relations. Training can be administered in a classroom, through a self-study manual, or by video. Workpaper 3-5 helps plan checkpoint review training sessions.

Task Two: Conducting the Background Review. The first step is to gather background information about the audit to understand IT, its importance to the business, and any areas of concern. Sources of information for background reviews include the following:

- Audit documentation
- Auditee manuals
- Correspondence
- Budgets
- Meeting notes
- Industry reports
- Government reports
- Current auditee operating statistics
- Internal auditors from last audit

The concerns uncovered from the background review should be documented on Workpaper 3-6. Each concern should be identified, including specifically where in the information system that concern affects processing. Then, the concern should be described, including its potential frequency and impact.

Task Three: Developing a Review Work Program. The next task is to select, revise, or develop detailed checklists to guide the review team. Exhibit 3-2 is a work program that defines this task. It includes the following:

- *Quality factors.* Those factors most critical to the success and quality of the project or system being reviewed.
- *Quality characteristics.* Those that can be measured during the audit process (i.e., at certain checkpoints-four checkpoints are suggested) that reflect whether quality is being adequately addressed.
- *Checklist* (to be developed by the review team). The evaluation criteria used to measure the contributor characteristics and the action steps required to perform the evaluation. Workpaper 3-7 is used to develop checklists using the characteristics listed in Exhibit 3-3.

Workpaper 3-4. Auditor Selection Matrix

Audit:								
	Potential Reviewer							
Quality Factors								
Accuracy and completeness								
Authorization								
Workpaper integrity								
Reconstruction								
Continuity of processing								
Service level								
Security								
Cost-effectiveness								
Audit objectives								
Compliance								

Workpaper 3-5. Training Plan Checklist

Audit:				
Topic	**Include (Y/N)**	**Teaching Method**	**Materials Used**	**Training Schedule**

Audit Methodology
  Process Overview
  Products Produced				

Principles of reviews
  Purpose
  Definitions
  Quality factors
  Checkpoints in the audit process				

The review process
  Steps
  Roles and responsibilities
  Administration				

Review skills
  Work program preparation
  Interviewing
  Listening techniques				

Audit overview
  Audit purpose
  Audit description or overview
  Audit team members
  Audit schedule				

Other topics:
  _____
  _____
  _____				

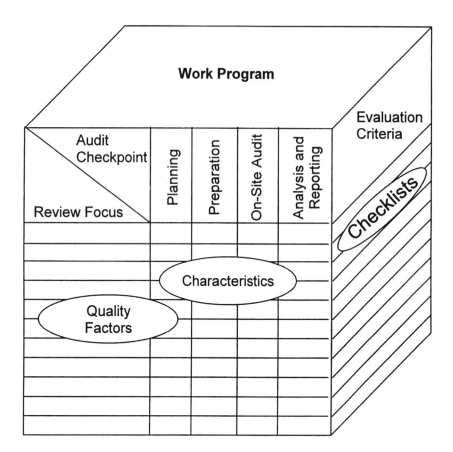

Exhibit 3-2. Three-Dimensional Work Program

The review team should develop a set of checklists before beginning each checkpoint review program. Exhibit 3-3 is a checklist representing areas to probe for each contributor characteristic for that audit checkpoint. For example, in audit review planning for the quality factor "accuracy or completeness," the questions should probe how accurate and how complete the audit effort must be (i.e., what accuracy and completeness tolerances have been established).

There are some guidelines for building a work program. Work programs should be actions for the work team to complete, not questions to be answered by the project team. Each item in the work program should require the reviewer to conduct an investigation to answer it. Reviewers should perform all of the items on the work program, but at their discretion they may make additional investigations. The review should improve the quality of the audit, and not pinpoint blame. The reviewer must clearly understand the difference between the quality factor (i.e., desired result) and the quality characteristic, which is the focus of a specific checkpoint review.

Exhibit 3-3. Example Characteristics

	Checkpoints			
Quality Factors	**Planning**	**Preparation**	**On-Site Audit**	**Analysis and Reporting**
Accuracy and Completeness	Tolerances established	Data controls defined	Data controls implemented	Verification of accuracy and completeness
Authorization	Authorization rules defined	Authorization method defined	Authorization method implemented	Data changes prohibited without consensus
Workpaper Integrity	Workpaper integrity requirements defined	Workpaper controls defined	Workpaper controls implemented	Verification of the integrity of the audit report
Reconstruction	Reconstruction requirements defined	Audit trail defined	Audit trail implemented	Reporting audit trail maintained
Continuity of Processing	Impact of failure defined	Contingency plan defined	Contingency plan written	Integrity of workpapers assured
Service Level	Desired service levels defined	Service method defined	Service methods implemented	Reporting schedules met
Security	Access defined	Security procedures defined	Security procedures implemented	Reporting security provided
Cost-Effectiveness	Calculated	Recalculated	Reevaluated	Analysis and reporting budget met
Audit Objectives	Measurable objectives defined	Audit approach achieves objectives	Programs achieve objectives	Problems identified in report
Compliance	Standards, policies, and procedures defined	Compliance methods defined	Compliance procedures implemented	Reporting procedures compliance

Workpaper 3-6. Background Review Concerns

Audit:	
Audit Quality Concern	**Description and Comments**

Workpaper 3-7. Work Program Checklist Development

Audit:	
Checklist #:	
Checkpoint or Phase:	
Quality Factor:	
Characteristic:	
Evaluation Criteria	**Review Test**

A checkpoint review planner should ask the following questions:

- Has quality assurance provided generic work programs for conducting reviews?
- Do those work programs apply to this review? If not, have checklists been customized for this review?
- Is the vocabulary adequate for this review?
- Does the reviewer understand all of the items in the generic work program?
- Is there adequate review time to do all of the items on the work program?
- Does the work program adequately address the intent of the quality factors applicable to this review?
- Have the review programs been allocated to specific individuals? If so, are those individuals qualified to conduct the checkpoint review?
- Will the reviewer have time to complete the review by the scheduled completion date?
- Are the reviewers trained in how to use the work program? If not, can training be provided in time to conduct the review?
- Will the reviews be completed in time to provide the project team with information to influence the project?

Workpaper 3-8 can be used to document the overall checkpoint review plan.

Step Three: Kick Off the Review Process

During this step the review chairperson assembles review materials and prepares the audit team for the review process, before the on-site audit. The review chairperson conducts a kick-off meeting with the review and project team to discuss review procedures, schedules, and assignments. It should involve all auditors, audit management, and appropriate auditees. The attendees should introduce themselves and explain their roles. The audit team should provide an overview of audit plans. Concerns should be voiced, and administrative issues (e.g., schedules, extra materials needed, who gets review reports) should be resolved. Workpaper 3-9 can be used to help prepare for the kick-off meeting.

Step Four: Reviewing the Project or the System

During this step, team members perform their work assignments for the current checkpoint review and document their findings. This step is performed at each scheduled project checkpoint. For systems of average size, the review process begins approximately two weeks before the checkpoint.

Workpaper 3-8. Checkpoint Review Plan

Audit		Audit Contact	Review Budget		Start Date	
Quality Factor	Checkpoint	Contributor Characteristic	Checklist No.	Reviewer Assigned	Schedule	Budget

Workpaper 3-9. Kick-off Meeting Checklist

Application System:				
Number	**Item**	**N/A**	**Date Completed**	**Completed by**
1	Set time, date, and location for meeting.			
2	Select and invite participants.			
3	Notify participants of their role in meeting.			
4	Ask audit management to attend and verbally support review effort.			
5	Prepare list of items expected from participants during review process.			
6	Prepare list of administrative requirements (e.g., work space, meeting space).			
7	Prepare meeting agenda.			
8	Prepare list of items for reviewers to cover during meeting.			
9	Brief reviewers before meeting.			
10	Appoint someone to take notes during the meeting.			

Task One: Optional Pre-Checkpoint Meeting. This meeting briefs the project team on checkpoint activities, hand out checkpoint review assignments, and clarify any concerns. If the chairperson opts to hold a checkpoint meeting, it should be the first task in a checkpoint review. The chairperson would usually hold this meeting if the following is true:

- The reviewers are new to the review process.
- It is the first checkpoint review for the audit.
- The reviewers are unfamiliar with the audit methodology or the business area being audited.
- The work performed during this checkpoint period is unusual, complex, or of critical importance to the organization.
- The chairperson believes it advisable to convene the team to improve team relationships. All review team members should attend the meeting.

A meeting normally lasts one hour or less. A tentative agenda for this pre-checkpoint meeting is as follows:

- Description of deliverables produced during this checkpoint period.
- Status of the audit.
- Status of audit deliverables.
- Overview of the project at this point (e.g., is it on schedule and within budget, what problems occurred, what did the audit accomplish during this checkpoint?).
- Distribution of review team assignments.
- Questions and answers about the audit and assignments.
- Summary and emphasis on when review work is to be accomplished.

Each review team member receives an assignment sheet and interview workpapers, as appropriate. The review chairperson completes one review assignment worksheet (see Workpaper 3-10) for each reviewer. The workpaper should include the following:

- Review dates
- Quality factors assigned to the reviewer
- Tools (e.g., work program checklists, questionnaires)
- Project materials used
- Estimated hours
- Assignment overview (what the reviewer is to do during this checkpoint)
- Review objectives (what the chairperson wants this person to accomplish during the checkpoint review)
- Comments (suggestions by the chairperson on the conduct of the review)

One workpaper is prepared for each individual or group to be interviewed during the checkpoint review (see Workpaper 3-11). This worksheet is completed partially by the chairperson and partially by the reviewer. The chair-

Workpaper 3-10. Checkpoint Review Assignment Sheet

Audit:		
Checkpoint or Phase:	**Review Schedule**	
Reviewer:	**Start:**	/ /
Quality Factor(s):	**Stop:**	/ /
	Estimated Hours:	
	Meeting:	/ /
Assignment Overview		
Tools		
Materials Used		
Review Objectives		

person contributes the administrative review data and the purpose of the review. Because several reviewers will be talking to different people, the chairperson must minimize overlap and duplication of interaction with specific individuals. The reviewer adds the results of the interview to the workpaper, including what the reviewer learned from the discussion and items for potential follow-up.

Task Two: Preparing for the Review. Each review team member must spend time preparing for the review. As a rule of thumb, the reviewer should spend about one-third of the time preparing, one-third of the time reviewing, and one-third of the time documenting the issues. The reviewer must do four things to prepare for the review:

- *Analyze audit documentation.* The reviewer should analyze the documents indicated on Workpaper 3-10 as needed for the review. The reviewer wants to determine the following:

    — The status of audit deliverables.
    — The status of the audit.
    — Turnover in audit staff.
    — Completeness of deliverables.

The reviewer should highlight material in the project deliverables relating to his or her assignment.

- *Plan the review.* The reviewer should determine what steps need to be taken to complete the review. These steps can include determining the following:

    — What additional documentation needs to be obtained.
    — Which individuals to talk to.
    — What work program task needs to be completed.
    — The adequacy of the schedule and budget.

- *Schedule interviews.* Their times and locations must be arranged.
- *Get familiar with the review work program.* The reviewer must understand all the tasks required and the questions to be answered during the review.

Task Three: Conducting the Review. Each review team member uses his or her specialized work program to investigate the quality factors he or she has been assigned to review. The reviewers must not simply follow the same path as the audit team.

Work programs contain questions the reviewer must answer, but not necessarily ask. Reviewers can use interviews, questionnaires, and documentation reviews to determine these answers. Reviewers who conduct interviews should try to do the following:

Workpaper 3-11. Interview Worksheet

Audit:	
Interview Place:	**Date:**
Person Interviewed:	
Department:	**Position:**

Purpose of Interview

Results of Interview

Items for Follow-Up				
Item	**Follow-Up Needed**	**Done by**	**Date**	**Result**

- Explain the purpose of the interview at interview opening.
- State how results of the interview will be used.
- Not criticize any actions performed by interviewee.
- Show empathy to interviewee's position.
- Always talk in positive terms.
- Attempt to summarize interviewee's statements but not draw conclusions from them.
- Request source of any factual data provided.
- Limit the interview to no more than one hour.
- Schedule interviews for a convenient time.
- At the end of the interview, summarize all of the key points that will be recorded as a result of the interview.
- For factual data, leave a questionnaire to be completed at the interviewer's convenience rather than asking for such factual data as, "How many records are processed a day by this application?"

Workpaper 3-11 can be used to record notes from an interview.

The following are some guidelines for using questionnaires:

- Questions on questionnaires are designed to be answered by the interviewer, not the interviewee. The interviewer must do enough investigation, probing, and questioning to understand answers to his or her questions.
- Open-ended questions tend to get more information than closed-end questions.
- It is best not to ask multiple questions about the same topic but, rather, to skip around to different topics. This will avoid channeling the interviewee's thinking.
- The interviewer should not ask questions unless he or she understands them.
- The interviewer should recognize the bias in the responses he or she is receiving, as the respondent wants to please and will often answer that a system is of high quality.

Task Four. Documenting Issues. This task identifies, during the review process, areas where the system or specifications do not adequately address a specific quality factor. These areas may be uncovered during the review, during the work program, or during analysis of review results. Three types of issues should be documented:

- Major issues:

  —Items whose impact can be quantified.
  —Items that would cause the audit to develop invalid findings or miss findings.

—Items that represent an error in the documented audit requirements or specifications.

- Minor issues:

   —Items that will significantly affect the audit.
   —Items with economic impacts that cannot be determined.
   —Small documentation errors or minor variances from standards.

- Unresolved issues:

   —Major concerns for which the facts are unavailable or the effects of which are unclear.
   —Items requiring additional investigation.
   —Items that cannot be addressed until future checkpoints.

Significant issues should be discussed both with the auditor in charge and at the review meeting. Minor issues should be given to the auditor in charge for resolution. Unresolved issues should be given to the review chairperson. It is important to notify the review team leader of issues as soon as they are uncovered. Ideally, all issues should be resolved before the review team meets. Issues should be documented in Workpapers 3-12A, 3-12B, and 3-12C.

Step Five: Conducting a Review Meeting

Review team members, reviewers, and project personnel reconvene after performing their individual review assignments to discuss their findings and agree on the review outcome. This occurs at each scheduled project checkpoint.

Task One: Drafting a Preliminary Report. The review chairperson and review team members document the key objectives to be accomplished by the report, the findings and magnitude of findings uncovered during the conduct of the review, and recommendations for dealing with those findings. Source documents for developing the report include Workpapers 3-12A, 3-12B, and 3-12C.

The report can be written as a bullet point list. It does not have to be written in narrative format but may be, at the discretion of the review chairperson and depending on the formality of the organization's review reporting process. The report is prepared in the following sequence (see Workpaper 3-13):

1. List all findings. (Follow-up and trivial items may be converted to report findings at the discretion of the chairperson.)
2. When all of the findings have been recorded, indicate the relative magnitude of the findings in three categories: high, medium, and low.

Workpaper 3-12A. Checkpoint Review Issues List of Minor Issues or Problems

Audit:			
Checkpoint or Phase:			
Reviewer:			
Number	Issue or Problem	Reason for Concern	Disposition

Workpaper 3-12B. Checkpoint Review Issues List for Unresolved Issues

Audit:			
Checkpoint or Phase:			
Reviewer:			
Number	**Open Issue or Question**	**Reason for Concern**	**Disposition**

Workpaper 3-12C. Checkpoint Review Issues List for Significant Issues or Problems

Audit:
Checkpoint or Phase:
Reviewer:
Finding:
Reason for Concern:
Impact of Issue:
Recommendation:
Workpaper Support:

Workpaper 3-13. Preliminary Checkpoint Review Report

Audit:					
Checkpoint or Phase:					
Report Objectives: 1. 2. 3. 4.					
Number	**Finding**	**Magnitude (low, medium, or high)**	**Accepted (Yes/No)**	**Recommendation**	**Accepted (Yes/No)**

3. Identify a recommendation for each finding.
4. When all the findings and recommendations have been documented, the chairperson assesses the impact and develops one to four report objectives or major events that the chairperson hopes to accomplish from this checkpoint review.

Task Two: Discussing Review Findings. The next task is for all reviewers to discuss the findings, issues, and corrective action taken so far by the audit team. Each reviewer summarizes his or her findings and recommendations. The chairperson reviews findings and recommendations one by one, and all reviewers should be allowed to discuss each finding or recommendation. The review team accepts or rejects the findings or recommendations. This can be done by a majority vote, two-thirds vote, full consensus, or at the discretion of the chairperson. This meeting can occur before the drafting of the preliminary report or after, just before the checkpoint review meeting.

Task Three: Conducting the Checkpoint Meeting. The next task is to present checkpoint review findings and recommendations, get agreement on the findings, and strive to get agreement on the recommendations. Modifications to the findings and recommendations may be made during this meeting. Workpaper 3-14 can assist in setting up the meeting. All reviewers should be invited. Project management and key participants (those affected by the findings and recommendations) should be invited. The review meeting date should be established when the review begins. Meeting notice can be formal, and the meeting should not exceed two hours.

The review chairperson should do the following to ensure a successful review meeting:

- Prepare an agenda for the meeting and distribute it to all attendees.
- Distribute the preliminary review report (Workpaper 3-13) to all attendees.
- Let the reviewer involved in conducting the review discuss the findings and recommendations.
- Encourage open discussion by all participants on each finding or recommendation.
- Concentrate discussion on the facts; the meeting should not be used as a working meeting.
- Record all unresolved issues on a follow-up issues worksheet (i.e., Workpaper 3-12B).
- Publish start and stop times. If work exceeds stop time, the meeting should be stopped and another meeting scheduled.

At the beginning of the review meeting, the review chairperson states objectives of the meeting. Then, the meeting should be organized by quality

Workpaper 3-14. Review Meeting Checklist

Audit:				
Checkpoint or Phase:				
Number	**Item**	**N/A**	**Date Completed**	**Completed by**
1	Set time, date, and location for meeting.			
2	Select and invite participants.			
3	Notify audit team members of their role in meeting.			
4	Prepare agenda for the meeting.			
5	Prepare list of findings that the audit team will verify.			
6	Prepare list of recommendations that the audit team will comment on, accept, or reject.			
7	Prepare sufficient copies of the preliminary report to distribute to meeting attendees.			
8	Appoint someone to record results of the meeting.			

factors, with team members discussing their findings and recommendations one by one within their quality factor area of responsibility. It is important to finish discussing each finding and recommendation before proceeding to the next finding and recommendation. At the conclusion of the meeting, the review chairperson should summarize its results and say that the next step will be to finalize and issue the report.

Step Six: Following Up

The review chairperson ensures that all review issues have been resolved, issues the final review report, and issues the final review report.

Task One: Issue the Report. The report documents the checkpoint review results and distributes this information to the involved parties. Checkpoint review reports should be given exclusively to the project team because

- the purpose of a review is to raise issues, not resolve them
- checkpoint reviews are a quality control tool, a project tool, not a management tool
- the project manager, not the review team, should run the project and make decisions
- this encourages support for reviews by the project team

Giving copies to other parties, particularly the project leaders' management, is a pressure tactic to get recommendations adopted and should be avoided.

The review team should not sign off on audits or in any other manner indicate an audit is acceptable. This is a decision exclusively of the auditor in charge. If there is a sign-off, the auditor in charge should provide it, based on the information supplied by the review team.

A recommended report outline includes the following:

1. Report Purpose.
2. Background.
3. Scope of Review.
4. Findings (with current status).
5. Conclusions.
6. Recommendations (with current status).
7. Project team comments.

The review chairperson should use report writer's checklist in Workpaper 3-15 as a guideline for effective report writing. He should provide time for team members to review the draft and make comments before issuing the report. The report should never name names or assign blame; instead, it should stress quality. It is best to limit the size of the narrative report to

Workpaper 3-15. Report Writer's Checklist

Criteria	Yes	No	N/A
Complete			
1. Does it give all necessary information?			
2. Is it written with the reader in mind, and does it answer all his or her questions?			
3. Is there a plan for a beginning, middle, and end?			
4. Are specific illustrations, cases, or examples used to the best advantage?			
5. Are irrelevant ideas and duplications excluded?			
6. Are the beginning and the ending of the report effective?			
Clear			
7. Are the ideas presented in the best order?			
8. Does each paragraph contain only one main idea?			
9. Does a new sentence start each main idea?			
10. Are thoughts tied together so the reader can follow from one to another without getting lost?			
11. Are most sentences active? Are the verbs mostly specific, action verbs?			
12. Is the language adapted to the readers; are the words the simplest that carry the thought?			
13. Is underlining used for emphasis, and parentheses for casual ideas?			
14. Do the report's words impart their intended meaning to the reader?			
Concise			
15. Does the report contain only essential facts?			
16. Are most of the sentences short?			
17. Are most paragraphs short?			
18. Are unneeded words eliminated?			
19. Are short words used instead of long ones?			
20. Are roundabout and unnecessary phrases eliminated?			
21. Are pronouns used instead of repeating nouns?			
22. Is everything said in the fewest possible words?			

Workpaper 3-15. Report Writer's Checklist *(Continued)*

Criteria	Yes	No	N/A
Correct			
23. Is the information accurate?			
24. Do the statements conform to policy?			
25. Is the writing free from errors in grammar, spelling, and punctuation?			
Tone			
26. Is it natural? Is the language of conversation used?			
27. Is it personal? Are the ìweî and ìyouî appropriately emphasized?			
28. Is it friendly, courteous, and helpful?			
29. Is it free from words that arouse antagonism?			
30. Is it free from stilted, hackneyed, or technical words and phrases?			
Effective			
31. Is there variety in the arrangement of words, sentences, and pages so that it is interesting to look at?			
32. Was it tested by reading it aloud?			
Conclusion			
33. Is the report satisfactory and ready for final publication?			

two to three pages that stress major items. Other information can be included in appendixes and schedules. Small problems should be eliminated from the report (the project leader can use Workpaper 3-12A to give these to the project people).

Task Two: Follow Up on Issues. The chairperson should, within one to two weeks after the checkpoint report has been issued, check with the auditor in charge to verify that action has been taken on the report findings or recommendations to determine whether the audit team has taken action on the review findings and recommendations and to follow up on unresolved issues. The chairperson should also ascertain that the audit action is acceptable. Unacceptable action should be recorded as follow-up items (see Workpaper 3-16). Then, the chairperson should continue to follow up with the responsible audit person on the follow-up action items. Items not properly resolved by the audit team should be addressed in the next checkpoint review.

Workpaper 3-16. Checkpoint Review Follow-Up Action

Number	Description of Outstanding	Item Action to be Taken

Chapter 4
Using Teams for Process Improvement

Using teams is one way to improve IT audit processes. These processes include annual audit planning, a process for individual audit planning, report writing, and audit staffing. The process owners and users are in the best position to improve them. They should form a quality improvement team to improve the process.

This section describes two distinct processes. The first is for establishing a quality improvement infrastructure, including the formation of effective quality improvement teams. The second is an eight-step quality improvement process. An integral part of it are the tools used to perform the improvement steps. Appendix A describes these tools, and Chapter 6 provides a process for building a toolbox for audit teams.

DEFINING PROCESS

A process is a work activity or a series of related work activities that support the production and delivery of a defined deliverable. A well-defined information technology (IT) audit process consists of the following:

- Standards that define what is expected when building IT audit products and providing services.
- Procedures that define how to produce and deliver according to professional standards.
- Automated and manual tools that support the standards and procedures.
- Hardware required to produce and deliver audit products.
- Quality control methods that help ensure that audit products and services conform to standards.

THE PURPOSE OF QUALITY IMPROVEMENT PROGRAMS

Quality improvement programs (QIPs) reduce the frequency of defects caused by ineffective audit processes. Without programs of this type, a cycle of uncovering product defects and then removing those defects from the product is continuous because the same defects may occur each time a product is built. The long-range objective of QIPs is to eliminate the need for such activities as audit reviews. If processes reliably generate zero defect results, there is no need to find and correct product defects.

Quality improvement involves finding defects, distinguishing the significant defects from the insignificant ones, selecting the most significant defect, and identifying its root cause. At that point, an action program is put into place to reduce the frequency of defects or eliminate the cause of the defect. Then, the process selects the next most significant defect and repeats the quality improvement process.

The following four principles are important in making a quality improvement program work:

- *Quality improvement results from management action.* Management must recognize the problem in quality and initiate a QIP to address that problem. Usually, the individual or group involved in producing the product has only minimal control over defects. Management action is needed because that individual or group does not control the processes.
- *Everyone involved must be a part of the QIP.* All functions, activities, and individuals involved in the defective product or process must be involved in its solution. Each individual need not personally participate in a group designed to reduce or eliminate the cause of the defect, but his or her counsel must be sought. These users must be involved in the solution process because the process will likely fail unless the users "own" the final quality improvement solution.
- *The strategy of zero defects must be fostered.* Both management and the participants in the QIP must strive for zero defects. They should investigate the cause of all defects in the products or processes under scrutiny and attempt to eradicate those causes.
- *The cost of quality associated with a defect must be known.* Both management and the QIP must strive to price the cost of poor quality to demonstrate the value of the changes proposed by the QIP.

The impediments to a QIP include the following:

- *Management feels that everything is OK.* Until people perceive a need for improvement, they will not support programs to improve matters.
- *The short-term, reactive approach.* There is always enough money to correct defects in operational systems, but there is never enough money to eliminate the root cause of those defects.
- *Misunderstanding the meaning of quality improvement.* Some may associate this with increased cost (i.e., quality means relative goodness).
- *If it works, leave it alone.* Many IT audit managers and staff do not want to spend money on something that already works. Although they recognize that there may be some benefit to making changes, they are not willing to accept the associated risk.

- *Lack of resources.* This reason for not taking action applies to almost any improvement program.
- *The customers or users control the system.* Many IT managers do not want to accept responsibility for modifying a system without customer approval or concurrence.

QIP CRITICAL SUCCESS FACTORS

The following are critical success factors for implementing a QIP. A quality improvement team infrastructure must address them:

- *Continual quality improvement.* This is the primary goal of a QIP. It requires a permanent, ongoing process that encourages and enables employees to improve their work processes.
- *Total employee involvement.* Achieving quality improvement requires 100 percent involvement. Everyone, from the top executive to the clerical support staff, must be included in the program.
- *Teamwork.* Teams, not individuals, ensure quality.
- *Senior management commitment.* A commitment to quality must start from the top. This requires management to show commitment through its actions.
- *Empowerment.* Management must listen to its employees. Management must also relinquish some control and give employees an appropriate level of decision-making authority. If management is willing to dole out responsibility, it must also be willing to dole out authority. Management must also support the speed and responsiveness of the problem-solving process. Management involvement often requires too much time. Problems can be solved and improvements implemented quickly if there is little intervention.
- *Rewards, recognition, and celebration.* Material incentives, recognition, and celebration acknowledging quality improvement are necessary to thank, honor, and motivate employees. They also contribute to something that is often overlooked: fun. Research indicates that morale is poor and enthusiasm is low when people generally do not have fun. Rewards, recognition, and celebration can revolutionize employees' attitudes about their jobs, the companies they work for, and most important, themselves.
- *Well-defined processes.* The key to quality improvement is to manage by process, continually striving to improve work processes. Every aspect of building, delivering, and maintaining an information system must have well-defined work processes to support it. A QIP must therefore have a well-defined infrastructure and supporting processes to address the QIP-critical success factors.

- *Measurement.* People cannot measure what they cannot control, and they cannot control what they cannot measure. Measuring quality improvement is necessary to evaluate quality improvement program effectiveness, communicate quality improvement progress, and determine when to say thank you with rewards, recognition, and celebration.
- *Communication.* Every employee must know everything about the QIP. It is imperative to have a well-defined method of communication.

A QIP INFRASTRUCTURE

A QIP infrastructure should contain six major components:

- A quality steering committee.
- Quality improvement teams.
- A quality improvement administrator or facilitator.
- A QIP measurement and reporting system.
- A QIP reward, recognition, and celebration program.
- A QIP communication system.

Exhibit 4-1 illustrates the relationship of the QIP infrastructure to the TQM infrastructure. A description of each infrastructure component follows.

Quality Steering Committee

In some organizations, the quality steering committee (QSC) is called the leadership committee. The QSC establishes and demonstrates commitment to quality improvement through the communication of visions and strategic plans. (The QSC may exist at several organizational levels, for example, at the enterprise level and at the audit level. Responsibilities may switch between levels in some organizations.)

The participants must include the audit director, all audit department heads, and the quality assurance manager. Their roles and responsibilities are as follows:

- *Lead the organization in recognizing the need and urgency for quality improvement.* Participants must demonstrate an active and involved commitment to continual process improvement. Initially, this consists of establishing a foundation on which to build the QIP by doing the following:

   —Determining what quality means to the participants, personally.
   —Determining what quality means to the organization.
   —Determining how to express the quality definition in clear and concise terms.
   —Communicating the quality definition to all employees.

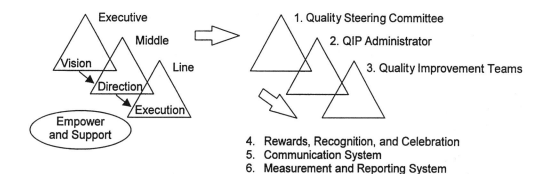

Exhibit 4-1. The Relationship of the QIP Infrastructure to the TQM Infrastructure

---

The importance of this initial task cannot be underestimated. The QSC must begin its leadership with a clear understanding of the task being undertaken and must communicate this understanding to all employees.

- *Promote and support quality improvement.* The QSC members must continually promote and support the QIP. Talking about quality improvement at every opportunity, periodically visiting QIP teams, or calling QIP team members to discuss implemented improvements are ongoing ways to do this.
- *Reward, recognize, and celebrate.* Whenever rewards are presented, recognitions given, or celebrations held, the QSC members must be involved. They must never delegate this responsibility. Presenting a reward, being photographed with a team for the company or departmental newsletter, kicking off a celebration with a short speech, or serving refreshments at a celebration are the types of activities in which the QSC members should participate.

Quality Improvement Team

Every member of the IT audit staff, from the audit director to the receptionists, must become involved in the QIP. Everyone does not have to be on a team, although auditors are encouraged to organize as many teams as practical. Two methods are recommended for creating the teams/workgroups.

Natural work groups characterize the way companies currently organize their work forces. A system development project team is a natural workgroup. This technique is recommended for initiating a QIP (see short-term plan). It is the easiest, quickest, and least-confusing method for organizing teams. Generally, these teams already exist, and the members have an established working relationship. In addition, they are usually aware of several ways to improve the effectiveness of their workgroup.

If natural work group teams elect to address problems that affect more than their team, the QIP should try to accommodate their effort, perhaps by including a process that allows multiple teams to collaborate and work together on projects that have a broader scope. Because the measurement system must track and report these instances, appropriate rewards and recognition must be given for these shared team efforts.

Using interdepartmental teams is a way to organize teams across departmental boundaries. They promote interdepartmental cooperation and help break barriers and problems within organizations. In addition, it is an excellent way to address problems that affect more than one workgroup or department. Because these types of problems are typically complex, it is also an effective way to organize mature QIPs.

Regardless of the method employed for organizing, each team should consist of five to eight members. Smaller or larger groups are acceptable, although effectiveness can be lost with too few or too many members.

Team member responsibilities should include the following:

- Identifying problems and selecting the ones to work on.
- Proposing solutions to problems.
- Choosing the appropriate solution and improvement approach.
- Implementing the chosen improvement.
- Presenting implemented improvement for certification that the QIP processes were followed.
- Documenting required data regarding team activities in the QIP measurement system.
- Ensuring consistent use of a common set of statistical process control tools and techniques.

Team members should be allocated at least one hour per week to meet and work with their teams. Teams should use this time to fit members' work schedules best. Because the entire work force participates, it is important to limit the time so as not to encroach on team members' daily responsibilities. However, if teams are trained in effective problem-solving and meeting-leading skills, this seemingly small amount of meeting time can be very productive, causing quality improvement and associated cost savings to soar.

The quality improvement team component addresses several critical success factors. It addresses teamwork with its emphasis on accomplishing quality improvement with teamwork. It addresses empowerment with teams allowed to implement improvement without involving management. It ensures total employee involvement with the participation of every employee required. It satisfies the requirement for continual quality improvement with teams meeting on an ongoing basis every week or every other week.

Quality Improvement Administrator

The quality improvement administrator is necessary to manage the QIP. This component ensures a daily focus upon the program. The administrator works first to build the QIP and then to facilitate the QIP group. The responsibilities of the quality improvement administrator (in a small organization, this may be a part-time responsibility) are as follows:

- Manage the QIP, handling its day-to-day operation. The administrator is constantly monitoring the QIP, identifying problems with the process, and ensuring that problems are addressed.
- Provide direction to the teams and ensure they receive proper training.
- Review and certify all implemented improvements. (This normally means ensuring the QIP team follows all the QIP processes and not actually validating results.)
- Compile QIP measurement statistics and report to all employees.
- Identify teams for reward and recognition based upon the reward system criteria and ensure that rewards and recognition are given.
- Schedule and organize periodic celebrations.
- Transmit or implement improvement ideas to other areas and activities that could benefit from them.

These seven administrator responsibilities do not adequately describe a successful administrator. They describe the tasks the administrator performs rather than the manner in which the administrator performs those tasks. The administrator should be a leader. He or she should define and explain the QIP vision, persuade the necessary people to accomplish the vision, and motivate those involved in the process. QIPs should support the audit vision. The administrator must clearly explain and describe that vision to the QIP team. The administrator must make sure that the activities performed by the QIP teams support that vision. The administrator must ensure that the appropriate people are on the team. If additional expertise is needed, the administrator must provide it or identify someone who can. However, the major leadership responsibility of the administrator is to motivate the QIP teams. It is easy for interest and excitement to ebb and flow over time. To assure that the teams are properly motivated, the administrator must do the following:

- Attend meetings and add encouragement during them.
- Ensure that management permits adequate time from the members' workdays to perform QIP tasks.
- Pitch in and help where appropriate, including acting as a facilitator at the QIP meeting.

- Maintain excitement for the program by providing a variety of activities, such as short-term contests, special awards, recognition days, and generally making the activity fun.

For each 500–600 team members there should be at least one full-time resource committed for administering and managing the process. However, regardless of the number of teams, no less than 10 percent of one person's time should be allocated to managing a QIP process.

The quality improvement administrator should be organizationally equivalent to at least a project leader. Ideally, the administrator would report directly to the IT audit director. The position should be staffed with someone who is enthusiastic and people-oriented and who possesses excellent oral and written communication skills. The person does not necessarily have to have audit experience but should be an experienced business person.

QIP Measurement and Reporting System

The QIP measurement and reporting system is necessary to gather, compile, and report QIP statistics to all employees (e.g., number of teams, improvements implemented, and savings from improvements). It should be an automated system easily accessible to all teams. Regardless of hardware involved, it must be simple and easy to use. Each team will be required to capture and enter into the system data regarding any improvement efforts. The system should have simple statistical reporting capabilities to enable the quality improvement administrator to provide comprehensive, accurate, and timely reporting.

The measurement and reporting system should maintain a history of improvements. Each improvement should be adequately documented, and the organizations affected by that improvement should be identified. The impact should be on organizational entities currently affected by the improvement as well as those that could be affected by the improvement. For example, if a QIP improvement idea assisted a programming group in the programming task, that same improvement idea could possibly help all programming groups. Through the measurement and reporting system, the administrator captures this history of improvement ideas. The administrator is then responsible for ensuring that those ideas are appropriately transmitted and/or implemented into other impacted areas.

Required data statistics for the QIP should reflect the type of information that management, team members, and customers would like to see. At a minimum, each improvement idea should include the following:

- Date improvement idea was selected.
- Date improvement idea started.
- Improvement team name or identification.

- Status of improvement—inactive, active, or implemented.
- Date improvement idea was completed.
- Cost savings associated with improvement.
- Date improvement idea was certified.
- Benefit realized by improvement.

This data quantifies several implemented ideas and cost savings because the industry trend in QIPs is to reward improvement ideas on either the total number of improvements or total cost savings of improvements. However, other measures are equally valid in assessing the QIP contribution, such as the following:

- Improved customer service.
- Improved customer satisfaction.
- Increased revenue to the organization.
- Improved morale of the IT audit staff.
- Reduced cycle time of building or maintaining IT audit products and services.

The measurement system should not require a major resource investment to implement. Usually, existing hardware and software can handle the simplistic data storage, compilation, and reporting requirements. However simple, the system is a very important and significant component of the QIP, addressing several critical success factors. Its reporting capabilities contribute to improved communication, and its improvement tracking capabilities help identify teams that deserve rewards and recognition.

QIP Reward, Recognition, and Celebration Program

The importance of a QIP reward, recognition, and celebration program cannot be overemphasized. It can make or break a QIP. No single type of reward, recognition, or celebration can address the various needs of employees. People want and need to be thanked in different ways. A QIP reward system should be flexible.

The specific rewards are not the most critical idea. What is critical is that they occur and that they occur systematically. Randomly occurring reward, recognition, or celebration events will not be successful.

A process should recognize quality improvement according to well-defined criteria. They must be consistent with the primary QIP objective. The organization must define and measure this objective. The number of implemented improvements should be the measure by which quality improvement is judged. Some organizations measure by cost savings or a combination of cost savings and number of improvements. However, recognizing quality improvement by measuring cost savings can create a perception that cost savings, not quality improvement, is the goal. In addition, some improvements may not generate an immediate or quantifiable cost savings, and those should not be overlooked. Several companies have successfully used cost savings with the number of improvements as a measure. However, in these organizations, the emphasis of the QIPs was always on quality improvement, not cost savings.

Whatever is used to measure quality improvement, specific levels of the measure should be the criteria for reward and recognition. They should represent milestones achievable within a reasonable amount of time. Predetermined rewards and recognition should be associated with each level. Organizations should be creative with their recognition efforts. In addition to rewards and recognition, celebrations should be regularly planned, either semiannually or annually, to celebrate quality improvement.

QIP Communication System

The QIP communication system helps keep all employees informed about the QIP. The system should handle regular and spur-of-the-moment types of communications. The types of information that must be communicated by this system include the following:

- *QIP objectives and goals.* This is critical during implementation and on an ongoing basis.
- *Team member and team leader roles and responsibilities.* This is critical information during implementation but is also very important on an ongoing basis.
- *QIPs.* Everyone must be constantly aware of the processes and changes to the processes that support the program.
- *Team reward and recognition.* Everyone needs to be informed as teams achieve various levels of improvement and are rewarded and recognized for their efforts.

The system can use existing mediums of communication, such as company newsletters and publications, departmental newsletters and publications, and electronic mail. It can also consist of new media, such as a quality newsletter devoted solely to the QIP or quality bulletins that publicize quality news flashes.

QIP SHORT-TERM PLAN

Improving quality requires long-term strategies and commitment. However, building a mature quality improvement process requires a firm foundation. Therefore, it is necessary to develop a short-term strategy to provide a framework and demonstrate success to enable a long-term effort to gain hold. In the short term, the emphasis is on developing and implementing an infrastructure, preparing and training the IT audit staff, building simple problem identification and problem-solving skill sets, and establishing the management's commitment. The short-term goals are discussed in the following sections.

Implementing a QIP Infrastructure

Developing an infrastructure and supporting process is critical to managing a QIP. Without one, improvement is ad hoc and inconsistent.

Training the Entire Staff

Awareness training that presents the infrastructure and describes roles and responsibilities must occur before the program begins. In addition, training that addresses simple problem identification and problem resolution methods and effective meeting leading build team-building skill sets that enable teams to solve problems. Everyone must receive awareness and skill set training.

Preparing an organization for complex problem solving over the long term requires management be trained to be directors, facilitators, and coaches. These skill sets are essential to effective problem solving. Management must be trained first in these skills to ensure that the organization is ready for, and committed to, continuous improvement.

Establishing Commitment and Gaining Support Among Management and Line Personnel

It is unreasonable to expect employees to embrace the idea of quality improvement teams. Most will be skeptical. Therefore, in the short term the goal is to move them from resisting the program to accepting it. As the QIP matures, the goal will be to move the employees from acceptance to enthusiasm.

Improving Process, Product, and Environment

The strength of a QIP lies in process improvement. Process improvement must be the primary goal. Initially, however, teams may choose to improve product or the environment. The latter should be encouraged, as improving the environment can positively affect employee morale. This is desirable and is important to establish acceptance in the short term.

The QIP administrator should direct the quality improvement teams to address small, easy-to-implement improvements. There are several reasons for this. First, these types of improvements are not insignificant. The cumulative effect of implementing small improvements is phenomenal. Quality improvement is accomplished one step at a time; the size of each step is not important. Second, the teams initially do not possess the skills necessary to solve complex interdepartmental problems. The skills will evolve in the long term with training and experience, but only after basic skills have been developed with simple problem solving.

Initially, quality improvement teams should be organized to address problems within natural workgroups. Natural workgroups focus on problems that affect their workgroup. Because these problems generally are simple and easy to identify and resolve, feedback and gratification is immediate. This feedback contributes to gaining support and establishing commitment, which is critical in the short term. Second, focused problem solving is ideal for practicing and improving problem-solving and team-building skills. In addition, integrating department personnel can introduce political factors that may initially inhibit problem-solving efforts. It is important to address these types of issues in the long term, but in the short term they can be overwhelming.

QIP LONG-TERM PLAN

In the long term, the emphasis is to build on the foundation established by the short-term plan. Long-term goals are described in the following sections.

Evolving the QIP Infrastructure

A fundamental tenet of quality improvement is continuous process improvement, both in the QIP infrastructure and in its supporting process. It is essential to improve the infrastructure to make it increasingly effective and successful.

Training Staff

The training and experience the staff received in the short term provides a solid base of problem-solving skills. The long-term focus is to build upon these skills and introduce new ones that will enable teams to identify and address complex problems. Statistical process control techniques should be introduced to create the skills that will allow the teams to measure, analyze, and identify problems with the existing work process. Cross-functional teams are required to solve these problems. This will demand effective direction and facilitation from middle management throughout the organization, which will require middle management and executives to use the skill set training they received in the short term, along with new skills developed by experience and additional training.

Enhancing Commitment and Support

The opportunities and success experienced in the short term generally motivate employees to accept QIP. That acceptance should grow into enthusiasm as skills are enhanced, improvements implemented, and rewards and recognitions received. As the organization's culture changes and employees realize that the QIP is a long-term commitment and not another program-of-the-month, enthusiasm for continued improvement opportunities will become permanent.

Improving Processes

Once quality improvement team members have been working as teams and solving simple problems within their workgroups for 12 to 18 months, they are ready to address complex interdepartmental problems. To do so, teams must be formed across functional areas. Interdepartmental problem-solving teams should be assembled and should involve all IT audit employees. The nature of interdepartmental problems involves issues that generally fall outside the scope of nonmanagerial team members. Therefore, managerial involvement is necessary and critical. Management must direct, lead, and facilitate these problem-solving efforts. They must not fall into their traditional roles of supervising and controlling but, rather, use the leader role of defining a vision, selecting the right team, empowering the team, and motivating the team to develop and implement improvements. The team members must still be empowered to improve processes; however, they require direction and leadership. Middle management must execute that role. Training received in the short term should have provided the skills required to fulfill those responsibilities.

The short-term and long-term plans are summarized in Exhibit 4-2.

AN EIGHT-STEP QUALITY IMPROVEMENT PROCESS

An eight-step continuous improvement process is presented as a flowchart in Exhibit 4-3. The first three steps focus on process identification and understanding; steps four through eight focus on process improvement. Each step is described in the following sections, and the tools typically used in each stage are listed. Exhibit 4-4 matches commonly used tools to the appropriate stages of the continuous improvement process. However, situations may arise in which additional tools are needed or the specified tool is not used.

Step One: Selecting the Process and Team

The process to be improved may be selected by the quality improvement team (QIT) or assigned to the QIT by management. The QIT is led by the process owner. QIP members come from those working in the process. Cross-functional QIT members are usually appointed by management. Organizational QIT members are usually volunteers. If subject experts are required and none volunteers, management may have to assign them. After

Exhibit 4-2. Quality Improvement Teams

Short Term	Long Term
1. Implement QIP infrastructure	1. Improve QIP infrastructure
2. Train staff and build awareness and skill sets • Infrastructures, roles, and responsibilities • Simple problem identification and resolution, team building, effective meeting • Management responsibility—directing problem-solving efforts	2. Train staff, improve skill sets to develop the full potential from QIPs. Includes such skills as • Statistical problem identification • Complex interdepartmental problem-solving potential
3. Establish commitment, gain support among middle and line personnel • Move from resistance to acceptance • Present how everybody will gain from the QIP	3. Enhance commitment and support • Move from acceptance to enthusiasm
4. Improve processes, products, and environment • Assemble teams according to existing natural workgroups	4. Improve processes • Assemble interdepartmental teams led and facilitated by management

the process has been selected and the QIT formed, the customer for the output of the process must be identified. Suppliers to the process are then determined. Representatives from the customers and suppliers should be on the QIT if practical. Often, the QIT begins by analyzing data on customer complaints, rework, scrap, and cost of quality. The quantitative tools used in this stage can include the flow, Pareto, and run charts.

Step Two: Describing the Process

Two simultaneous actions are initiated in this step: defining customer-supplier relationships and determining actual process flow. The process customer's requirements are defined using operational definitions to ensure complete understanding between the supplier and the customer. The customer's quality characteristics are defined, and the current state of satisfying these is determined. Meaningful specifications are documented that state the customer's expectations. In most instances, the customer referred to is the internal customer. This same idea is applied to the suppliers. The process owner's expectations are defined for suppliers of inputs to the process. The customer and supplier must then agree on the specifications to be met and how quality will be measured.

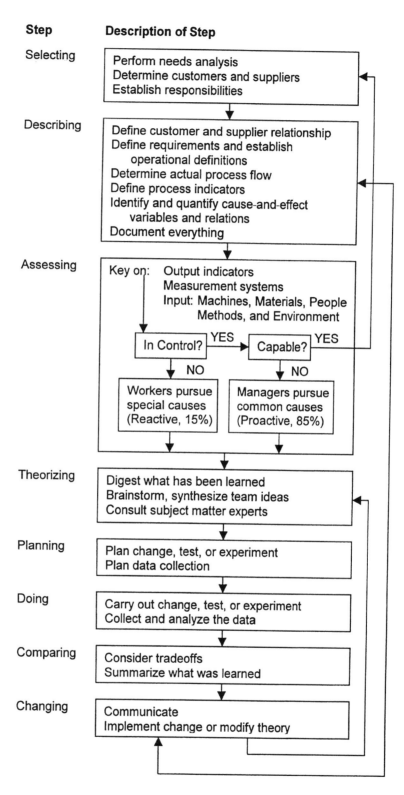

Exhibit 4-3. Flowchart of Eight-Step Continuous Improvement Process

Exhibit 4-4. Tools Used in the Continuous Improvement Strategy

Statistical Tools	Strategy Stages							
	Select	Describe	Assess	Theorize	Plan	Do	Compare	Change
Flowchart	●	●		●	●			●
Pareto chart	●	●	●	●			●	
Cause-and-effect diagram		●	●	●		●		
Scatter diagram and correlation		●		●		●		
Measurement and survey methods	●	●	●	●	●	●	●	●
Run chart	●	●	●	●		●	●	●
Histogram, normal distribution, and summary statistics		●	●	●		●	●	
Control charts: an introduction and illustration		●	●	●	●	●	●	●
Process capability			●	●	●	●	●	
Statistical experiments: illustration			●	●	●	●	●	

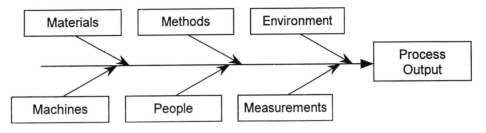

Exhibit 4-5. Cause-and-Effect Diagram

While the customer-supplier relationships are being defined, the team is building the "as is" flowchart of the process if one was not completed in the previous step. This details how the process is done at that point in time. Questions the team asks include the following: Does the person do the process the same way every time? Does each person, if more than one does the process, do it the same way? Is there variation from shift to shift? The flowchart identifies sources of variation and other causes of poor quality or productivity. The team uses the flowchart, along with discussions with the customer, to determine process measurement points, which monitor process input and output. Data that should be collected and analyzed is identified. A discussion of the ideal way to do the process is initiated: Is there a better, more efficient way to perform the process?

The initial cause-and-effect diagram should also be constructed in this stage (see Exhibit 4-5). A team brainstorming session is usually used to identify all possible causes of process input variation. These are then categorized, typically into measurement, methods, materials, machines, people, and environment. A separate cause-and-effect diagram is constructed for each effect. The team can use scatter diagrams to establish the relationship between each of the major causes of variation and the process output. Tools used in this step include measurement and data collection methods, flowcharts, Pareto charts, cause-and-effect diagrams, and scatter diagrams.

Step Three: Assessing the Process

To ensure that team makes decisions using precise and accurate data, the measurement system for assessing the process must first be evaluated. Is there a calibration and metrology system? Is it followed? Have gauge studies been performed to determine measurement variation? If test equipment is used, have equipment capability studies been completed? If the measurement is counting, as done in many white-collar applications, care should be taken to assure everyone is counting the same things in the same manner. Once it has been determined that the present measurement system does accurately describe the data of interest, baseline values for output and input measures should be established. Examples of process output indicators are as follows:

- Amount of rework.
- Errors, or defects, in audit products, reports, or services.
- Cycle time.
- Timeliness.
- Number of schedules missed.
- Changes per document.
- Absenteeism.

Process inputs, determined in step two, represent possible sources of variation that must be quantified. Process inputs and outputs can be baselined using any of the tools mentioned previously. The cause-and-effect diagram developed in the previous step should be reviewed and updated.

The process is next assessed for statistical control by constructing control charts for each of the important process inputs. If points are found outside the control limits because of special causes of variation, these must be investigated and control mechanisms installed in higher-level processes to eliminate them in the future. Data gathering continues to confirm the elimination of the special causes. The QIT may have to proceed to steps four through eight to find and eliminate the special causes of variation. Once the data points consistently remain within the control limits, the process is stable and, therefore, in a state of statistical control. The next assessment determines whether the process can meet audit expectations. The tools available for this stage are the same as those mentioned previously.

Description of Process Variation, Common and Special. Variation is common to all processes. One of the challenges of implementing TQM is to get those working in the process thinking of variation sources. How much of the observed variation can be attributed to measurements, methods, material, machines, people, and the environment? These potential sources of variation form the cause portion of the cause-and-effect diagram shown in Exhibit 4-5. If those working in or on the process can recognize sources of variation, they can help reduce the variation. This is the essence of continuous process improvement. Although process variation cannot be completely eliminated, it can be significantly reduced.

Consistency in all the processes from conception through delivery of a product or service is the cornerstone of quality. Paradoxically, the route to quality is not just the application of statistical process control and the resulting control charts. Managers must change the way they manage. They must use statistical methods to improve management processes as well as all other processes in the organization.

Special and Common Causes of Variation. Special causes of variation are not typically present in a process. They occur because of special or unique circumstances. If special causes of variation exist, the process can easily be unstable and unpredictable. Special causes must be eliminated to bring a process into a state of statistical control.

The strategy for eliminating special causes of variation includes the following:

- Working to get very timely data so that special causes are signaled quickly; that is, using early-warning indicators throughout an operation.
- Immediately searching for a cause when there is a signal that a special has occurred.
- Not making fundamental changes in that process but instead seeking ways to change some higher-level system to prevent that special cause from recurring.

Common causes of variation are normally found throughout a process and will vary in significance. The sum of these causes determines the magnitude of the process' inherent variation from the control limits. The common causes of variation include process inputs and conditions that regularly contribute to the variability of process outputs.

Each common cause typically contributes a small portion to the total variation in process outputs. The aggregate variability due to common cause has a nonsystematic, random-looking appearance. Because common causes are regular contributors, the process or system variability is defined in terms of them.

Strategies for reducing common causes of variation include the following:

- Talking to local employees, other managers, and staff from various functions.
- Improving measurement processes if measuring contributes to the observed variation.
- Identifying and ranking categories of problems by Pareto analysis.

Bringing a process into a state of statistical control and reducing variation due to common causes is process improvement and the real essence of continuous process improvement.

Tampering is any temporary adjustment to a process (typically by operator or machine) in response to a variation. By definition, process variation within control limits is expected and is not a reason for adjusting or changing the process. Managers who do not understand variation ask time and time again for explanations or corrective action when they confront variation within agreed-upon control limits.

Process management combines the power and knowledge of quantitative methods with employee involvement to continuously improve processes. The manager who owns the process to be improved is responsible for process management. His or her role is to lead the effort to improve the process. The leader focuses the team on identifying and reducing variation, as well as ensuring that cost-effective improvements are implemented. Each leader is responsible for identifying internal customers and defining their requirements. The leader must also make sure all improvements are documented and quantified. This is crucial to TQM success.

Step Four: Theorizing for Improvement

The team should review all relevant information, including the process flow-chart and cause-and-effect diagrams. A brainstorming session may be held to generate ideas for reducing input variation. It may help to visualize the ideal process. The what, how, and why of the improvement should be documented so everyone agrees to what will be done.

Step Five: Planning an Experiment to Test the Theory

A plan for conducting an experiment to test the theory developed in the preceding step is developed here. This process improvement plan specifies what data is to be collected, how it should be collected, who will collect the data, and how the data will be analyzed after collection. The statistical tools to be used for analysis are defined. Attention is given to designing data collection forms that are simple, concise, and easy to understand. These forms should be tested before being used. The process improvement plan is a formal document approved by the QIT at a team meeting. The tools used during this step include data collection methods, flow charts, control charts, process capability, measurement capability, scatter diagrams, and advanced statistical techniques.

Step Six: Performing the Experiment and Analyzing the Results

This step consists of carrying out the plan developed in the preceding step. The required data is collected using the forms previously tested. The data is then analyzed using the statistical tools decided on in the previous step. The process improvement plan is reviewed at QIT meetings to track progress on process improvement. Techniques usually used include run charts, histograms, measurement capability, control charts, and advanced statistical techniques.

Step Seven: Comparing Results with the Theory

This step uses the same statistical tools that were used in step three to compare the results of the experiment with that predicted in step four. Has the process been improved? Do the experimental results agree with scientific or engineering theory? If the results are not as expected, can they be explained? When results are not as expected, something can still be learned about the process and its variation. This is not a failure. The new information will be used to develop a new theory. Care should be taken to document lessons learned and accomplishments. A set of before-and-after Pareto charts, histograms, run charts or control charts are generally used in this step.

Step Eight: Changing the Process or Theory

If the results are not as expected, a new theory for improvement, based on what was learned, must be developed by returning to step four. If the results are as expected and are deemed practical and cost-effective, the change recommended in the process improvement plan is implemented. The implementation should be foolproof and monitored to ensure that the gains made in reducing variation are maintained.

The team then returns to step two to re-establish the process documentation. A decision is now necessary: Should the team continue to improve this process by further reducing variation due to common causes or start working on another process that does not meet customer requirements? The answer will probably be based on an economic analysis. If it is economically desirable to continue to reduce the process variation, the team develops another improvement theory and repeats steps four through eight. If it decides to improve a different process, the team goes back to the first step and applies all steps to the new process.

Why Process Improvement Fails

Teams and organizations that proceed directly from step four to eight without validating their theory with experimentation usually fail. They rarely get at the root variation and have no scientific reason for changing a process. They have not established causality between the change implemented and long-term variation reduction. Unfortunately, the jump from step four to step eight is so tempting that many teams make the leap. Teams and management want action and results now. Thus, they succumb to their desire to change a process without having a basis in knowledge.

Chapter 5
Selecting, Building, and Managing Teams

This section offers tips on selecting team members, selecting a team leader, creating team synergy, team building, and managing teams. The material is limited because there are many good books and publications on team building. This section provides some practical advice from the experiences of team members.

SELECING TEAM MEMBERS

The team is composed of many members. It is important to view a team as a totality and not be overly concerned about specific team members. For example, an individual weak in a specific skill or trait can be complemented by another team member strong in that skill or trait. Team organizers should look for a mix of people whose composite skills and traits can accomplish their assigned tasks.

Generally, a team member should do the following:

- *Be a self-starter.* Empowered teams do not have supervisors to direct them. People must create their own energy and enthusiasm to start and complete tasks.
- *Be a good communicator.* Teams generally operate under a consensus mode, requiring team members to communicate their feelings and ideas effectively.
- *Be a team player.* Team members must work for the good of the team and not the good of the individual. They must believe that if the team wins, the members win.
- *Be motivated.* Members must have enough motivation to keep sustained interest in the work tasks to ensure their timely and successful completion.
- *Want to learn.* Teams constantly look for new and better ways to complete tasks. They seek new ideas, new tools, and new approaches. Team members must be willing to learn and use new concepts.
- *Understand team tools and processes.* Team members need to follow team processes, such as quality improvement processes, and use such tools as affinity diagrams. Ideally, team members possess skills in those areas.

SELECTING A TEAM LEADER

Team leaders can be appointed but are better elected by the team members. The director may appoint a leader just to get the team established and develop synergism. At that point, the team can determine its method of operation and its leader.

Generally, a team leader needs all the traits of a good team member and should:

- *Be a facilitator.* The team leader is not a supervisor but is the one who accepts responsibility for making the team successful.
- *Not be overpowering.* The team leader cannot force his or her will on the team but, rather, must enable the team to operate as a unit.
- *Be organized.* Because the leader must ensure that tasks are completed and that information is properly disseminated, he or she must be able to meet schedules and ensure that tasks are completed.
- *Not be judgmental or defensive.* The leader must accept any and all suggestions or ideas without negatively judging their source. Likewise, the team leader should not be defensive about his or her positions but, rather, be willing to explain and negotiate, as appropriate.

TEAM LEADER RESPONSIBILITIES

The prime responsibilities of a team leader are to do the following:

- Train team members in team procedure and tools.
- Develop or improve team processes.
- Assist teams.
- Certify improvements. The team leader must ensure that improvements are adequately substantiated and communicated to individuals who have a vested interest in the success of the team efforts.

HOW TO CREATE TEAM SYNERGY

Teams are always more effective than the best individual in the team. There are many exercises that groups can do to illustrate that point. For example, if several people who saw a list of 20 items were asked to write down the 20 items, most would get only about eight. On the other hand, the combined ability of the group to remember the 20 items may produce a list of all 20 items, or close to it. To be effective, synergy must occur within a team. Synergy is one team member inspiring additional insight and ideas in another team member. This creates better ideas and solutions than the best person in the group could create by himself or herself. Exhibit 5-1 shows how to create positive and negative synergy in a group.

Exhibit 5-1. How to Create Team Synergy

Positive synergy
• Focus on tasks, not people
• Select the right mix
• Use the word "it" and not people's names
• Do not be judgmental
• Involve the entire group
• Seek confirmation on actions
• Be quiet until you have something worth saying
• Acknowledge group help and identified defects
• Help accomplish job
• Accept what is said by the speaker as true
• Do not discuss team activities afterwards
Negative synergy
• Be overpowering
• Be disorganized
• Use personal pronouns (e.g., you, he, she, we) to assign blame
• Debate matters
• Be defensive
• Communicate negative emotions (wait one day before doing this)

MEASURING TEAM MEETING EFFECTIVENESS

Team meeting effectiveness can be subdivided into meeting maintenance and group dynamics. Although most team leaders have previous experience in leading meetings, their skills may need improvement. Skill in group dynamics might also need improvement. The team leader needs sufficient skills, knowledge, and practice to become proficient in both requirements. Elements for meeting both maintenance and group dynamics should be developed into a team meeting effectiveness checklist that teams can use to evaluate themselves.

Teams should contribute to the development of the team meeting effectiveness checklist. Self-evaluation is nonthreatening and immediate. An example of such a checklist is found in Exhibit 5-2. Importance should be placed on the use of agendas, minutes, project reports, and process improvement plans. These simple tools, if used regularly, will help any team improve its effectiveness. Emphasis should also be placed on member participation, resolving conflicts, and creativity.

A point can be given for each yes answer, allowing the teams to track their progress. A team should use this checklist at each meeting to help members see how well they conduct their meetings. A team checking 20 yes responses (out of 29) can reduce how often they meet every month. The checklist should be completed at the end of the meeting. For the first several meetings, everyone should complete the checklist. Then, the team or team leader and facilitator can complete it.

Another way to evaluate team meeting effectiveness is to have a third party conduct the evaluation. This is usually not as effective as self-evaluation because it can be threatening to the teams and may not be timely.

Exhibit 5-2. Checklist for Evaluating a Meeting's Effectiveness

Activity	Yes	No
1. A meeting was held as scheduled or a reschedule note was issued.		
2. A written agenda was followed for the meeting.		
3. Assignments with target dates were made during the meeting.		
4. Tasks were shared equally by all members.		
5. Participation by all was balanced and equal.		
6. Project reports were made.		
7. Process improvement plans were updated.		
8. The meeting leader demonstrated a participative style by involving all members in appropriate discussion and decision-making.		
9. The leader demonstrated patience.		
10. The meeting started on time.		
11. The meeting ended on or before time.		
12. Resource people were present as scheduled.		
13. An attitude of responsibility for team success was shown by all members.		
14. Conflicts or misunderstandings were successfully resolved.		
15. There was an energetic and positive attack of the process or project.		
16. Road blocks to progress were removed when encountered.		
17. Appropriate problem-solving techniques were used, including training in new techniques when needed.		
18. The minutes of the last meeting were read at the beginning of the meeting.		
19. The agenda for the next meeting was prepared at the end of the meeting.		
20. Meeting space was available and set up before the meeting.		
21. Equipment and supplies were available for a productive meeting.		
22. Attendance records were posted.		
23. Visual aids were effectively used.		
24. Creativity enhancements were used.		
25. The meeting had a specific purpose.		
26. The meeting ended with members evaluating the meeting.		
27. The leader maintained or enhanced the members' self-esteem.		
28. The leader kept the focus on process improvement.		
29. The team made progress.		
30. The meeting was (select one): Productive		
OK, but could have been improved		
Unproductive		

Chapter 6
Building a Team Toolbox

This section provides a seven-step process to follow in building a toolbox for use by audit teams. The teams should select only the tools they need to perform their tasks. Several figures are provided that cross-reference the tools to their specific uses.

STEP ONE: SELECTING AND BUILDING A TOOLBOX

The most commonly used statistical and team tools are described in Appendixes A and B. They are the tools most closely associated with quality improvement processes in industry. For quality improvement to work, team members need the necessary tools to perform the improvement tasks and training to gain proficiency in tool usage.

The tools selected will be based on the specific tasks assigned to the audit teams. The most common tasks and the tools associated with those tasks are as follows:

- *Using quality improvement teams.*
- *Improving a defined audit process.* Exhibit 6-1 shows what tools are most effective in identifying, clarifying, and analyzing a defined audit process.
- *Improving an undefined audit process.* Exhibit 6-2 shows what tools are most effective in identifying, clarifying, and analyzing an undefined audit process.
- *Identifying the root cause of an audit process problem.* Exhibit 6-3 shows what tools are most effective in identifying, clarifying, and analyzing an audit process problem.
- *Using statistical analyses.* Exhibit 6-4 shows what statistical tools are most appropriate to the steps involved in any analytical process or process improvement process.
- *Conducting surveys and interviews.* Gathering information through surveys and interviews is an essential part of team work. Appendix C compares the two approaches and describes how to effectively execute a structured interview.
- *Team tools.* Exhibit 6-5 shows what tools are most effective in identifying, clarifying, and analyzing team tools.

Exhibit 6-1. A Toolbox for Improving a Defined Audit Process

	Identify	**Clarify**	**Analyze**
Tool	Flowchart	Run chart	Control chart
What	Shows process steps	Measures output	Statistical method Common or special cause
When	Understanding Show redundancy by teams	How process works Determine trends Detect changes	Define process Quantify variability Determine stability Predict performance

Exhibit 6-2. TQM Toolbox for Improving an Undefined Audit Process

	Identify	**Clarify**	**Analyze**
Tool	Brainstorming	Pareto voting or chart	Histogram
What	Generate ideas	Illustrate significant potential causes	Measure occurrence of repeated events
When	Start on a problem Creative new approaches	Identify most important causes Prioritize what to work on first	Display distribution of data Insight on variation of a process

Exhibit 6-3. TQM Toolbox for Identifying the Root Cause of an Audit Process Problem

	Identify	**Clarify**	**Analyze**
Tool	Affinity diagram	Cause-and-effect diagram	Force field analysis
What	Categories to create order out of chaos	Identify possible causes of a problem	Identify driving and restraining forces
When	Simplify data focus on key areas	Seek out root causes of a problem	People of the organization

The following three tasks can then be used to select tools:

- *Task One: Inventory current tool usage.* Determine what tools the audit organization uses to manage and monitor processes and products.
- *Task Two: Benchmark against other audit organizations.* Determine what other audit organizations include in their team toolboxes.
- *Task Three: Select the tools for the audit team toolbox.* Determine which tools are most appropriate for the team tasks based on the charts provided in this section, the inventory of current tools used, and the results of benchmarking against other organizations.

STEP TWO: DEVELOPING TOOLBOX TRAINING

This step determines the extent of training needed for the audit team members to become proficient in the team toolbox and who should be trained. The level and extent of training depends on the skills the team members are expected to develop.

Some of the training decisions to be made are as follows:

• Who will develop the training?
• Who will provide the training?
• Who needs awareness training and who needs skills training?
• When will the training will be offered?
• What training will be needed to keep skills proficient after initial training?

STEP THREE: MARKETING A TOOLBOX

Toolbox users and their managers must believe that there are tools essential to the effective use of teams. They must understand the need and use of tools and the expected benefits from them. Audit managers must buy in to the use of tools for two purposes: to provide the necessary resources for building the toolbox and training, and to allow team members the time necessary to use the tools. The users must be convinced that using the tools will significantly improve their team tasks.

STEP FOUR: INTEGRATING TOOLS INTO AUDIT WORK PROCESSES

Tools must be integrated into the work process. In other words, the auditor must need the tool to complete the work process. If the tools are left as optional considerations, their usage deteriorates. Integrating tools into the work processes means developing work procedures that incorporate tool usage. Chapter 4, which addresses using tools for process improvement, incorporates this concept.

STEP FIVE: CERTIFICATION

Some effort must be undertaken to evaluate or certify the proficiency of

• workers in using the tools
• effective integration of tools into the work process
• evidence that the tools were used effectively in performing the work process

This certification can be done by the team as self-certification or as part of the audit quality assurance function.

Exhibit 6-4. Where Statistical Tools Are Used

Statistical Tools	Steps					
	Define Process	Define Measures	Collect Data	Identify Opportunity	Improve Process	Measure Results
Pareto principle (Separate vital few)	●	●	●	●		●
Cause-and-effect diagram (Possible causes of problems)	●			●	●	
Checksheet (Gather, record, and format data)			●		●	●
Control charts (Monitor process and variation)	●	●	●	●	●	●
Histograms (Display frequency of occurrence of data)	●	●	●	●	●	●
Run charts (Track data for process activity, shifts, or trends)		●	●	●	●	●
Scatter plots (Display relationship between variables)	●	●	●		●	

Exhibit 6-5. Where Team Tools Are Used

Team Tools	Steps					
	Define Process	Define Measures	Collect Data	Identify Opportunity	Improve Process	Measures Results
Consensus (Accepting an agreed-on resolution)	•	•	•	•	•	•
Affinity diagram (Grouping language data)	•	•				
Benchmarking (Relative performance or best practices)		•	•	•		
Brainstorming (Creative ideas)		•	•	•	•	
Nominal grouping (Ranking ideas)		•	•	•	•	
Flowchart (Sequential steps of a process)	•			•	•	
Force field analysis (Driving or restraining forces)			•	•		
Matrix Data analysis (Relationships of two variables)	•		•	•		
Software quality deployment (Needs into operational deliverables)	•	•	•	•	•	•

STEP SIX: RECOGNITION AND REWARD

Many believe that team efforts are an integral part of an individual's job performance. However, experience has shown that teams need to be rewarded just as individuals are rewarded. These rewards should include both recognition and reward. Teams should be recognized for using quality tools to solve problems and improve their processes. They should be rewarded for using quality tools with such things as off-site daytime activities, team pictures with appropriate management, family or team picnics, and tickets to special events.

STEP SEVEN: CONTINUOUS IMPROVEMENT

Each process in the audit function must be continually improved to ensure productivity and quality gains. The process of building and implementing a toolbox also needs continual improvement. Once this process has been defined and installed in an audit, it should be subject to the continual process improvement steps described in this manual.

Appendix A
Team Toolbox: Pareto Principle and Analysis

Vilfredo Pareto, an Italian economist, found a large percentage of wealth was concentrated in a small portion of the population. He advanced the theory of logarithmic law through the study of the wealth distribution. Joseph Juran used the Pareto principle to describe any bad situation, as one tends to do for quality. Juran refers to this principle as the separation of the vital few from the trivial many, or the 80-20 rule.

In problem solving, especially problem identification, using the Pareto principle should be commonplace to seek out the few vital causes of a problem. This practice is essential for identifying major problems with any processes. All levels of management need to practice and master this tool. Two types of Pareto analysis are practiced: Pareto charts and Pareto voting.

PARETO CHARTS

A Pareto chart provides a special type of bar chart to view causes of a problem in order of severity—largest to smallest. It is an effective tool to graphically show where significant problems or causes are in a process. A Pareto chart can be used when data is available or can be readily collected from a process. Use of this tool occurs early in the process when there is a need to rank causes by frequency. Teams can focus on the vital few problems and the respective causes that contribute to these problems. This technique provides the ability to do the following:

- Categorize items, usually by content or cause. Content includes type of defect, place, position, process, and time. Cause includes materials, equipment, operating methods, personnel, and measurements.
- Identify the characteristics that most contribute to a problem.
- Decide what to work on first.
- Understand the effectiveness of the improvement by doing before-and-after improvement charts.

A Pareto chart is constructed by doing the following:

1. Listing the problems or causes worth investigating.
2. Collecting data (a checklist or tally sheet may be useful).

3. Determining the data classifications or groups.
4. Determining the percentage of the total that is assigned to each data classification.
5. Drawing the horizontal and vertical axis lines of the diagram.
6. Plotting a scale of amounts that fit the total of all the data classifications to be graphed on the left-hand axis.
7. Plotting a 0–100 percent scale, with 100 percent directly across from the largest data value on the right-hand axis.
8. Drawing in the columns or bars for each data classification and labeling each one.
9. Plotting the cumulative percentage and label.

PARETO VOTING

The Pareto voting technique identifies significant potential causes of a problem when the problem cannot be quantified. It can be used to obtain the vital few. A Pareto chart can be used to find quantifiable causes. Like a Pareto chart, Pareto voting is based upon the Pareto principle—20 percent of the causes creating 80 percent of the problems will be 80 percent of the group. Pareto voting is usually used with a cause-and-effect, or fishbone, diagram. Management teams that have implemented a TQM process often use this technique. However, any team can use this tool to separate the vital few causes from the trivial many as a means of ranking.

The steps for using this tool are different than Pareto charting, but with the same result: the identification of the most critical causes of a problem. The result is working on the right things first. The following steps are used:

1. Brainstorm potential causes of a problem (see Workpaper A-1).
2. Determine the total number of brainstormed ideas and multiply by 20 percent. (For example, ten ideas result in two.) If the result is a fraction, round up to next whole number.
3. Based on the results of step two, determine the number of votes each team member receives (see Workpaper A-2). In this case, each team member receives two votes.
4. Each team member then uses his or her allocated votes (two in this case) to select the causes that have the largest impact on the stated problem.
5. Tally the votes each cause receives. Those receiving the most votes are considered most important to the team.
6. Determine the plan of action to resolve these causes.

Pareto voting can be used to determine questions to ask customers or employees on satisfaction surveys, to understand why efforts to encourage quality are or are not working, and to choose areas or courses for training.

Workpaper A-1. Results of Brainstorming Potential Causes

Item	Frequency	%

Workpaper A-2. Problem Ranking

Problem	Problem ranked by			Final Action Ranking
	Frequency	Severity	Customer's View	

CAUSE-AND-EFFECT DIAGRAMS

Cause-and-effect diagrams are useful tools to visualize, clarify, link, identify, and classify possible causes of a problem. They are sometimes referred to as a fishbone, or characteristics diagrams. The technique keeps teams focused on a problem and potential causes. A diagnostic approach for complex problems, this technique begins to break down root causes into manageable pieces of a process. A cause-and-effect diagram visualizes results of brainstorming and affinity grouping through major causes of a significant process problem. Through a series of "why" questions on causes, this process can help discover a lowest-level root cause.

Developing a cause-and-effect diagram involves the following steps:

1. Generally, during a brainstorm session a problem (effect) is identified with a list of potential causes.
2. On the far right side of a piece of paper, someone writes this problem.
3. Major causes of the problems are added; they become big branches.
4. The results of brainstorming or affinity diagraming fill in the small branches (see Exhibit A-1).
5. The process continues until the lowest level subcause is identified.
6. After a team completes a fishbone diagram, someone must verify that the causes it cites strongly affect the problem being examined.
7. The most important causes should be selected first for work. Nominal grouping or the Pareto voting technique may be used to reach consensus.
8. Root causes by collecting appropriate data (i.e., sampling) to validate a relationship to the problem.

A cause-and-effect diagram provides a visual relationship between cause and effect. It breaks down a problem into a manageable group of root causes and separates the symptoms of a problem from the real causes. It also uses

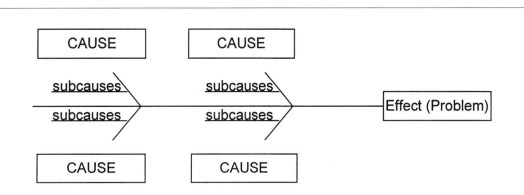

Exhibit A-1. Cause-and-Effect Diagram

teamwork to analyze problems. Cause-and-effect diagrams can help with the following:

- Problems analysis.
- A source for potential process improvements.
- A source of defect causes.
- The improper use of test routines or testing problems.
- Scheduling problems or cycle times.
- Compliance to or implementation of standards.

CHECK SHEETS

A check sheet is a form to gather and record data in an organized manner to help determine how often an event occurs over a specified interval of time. It is often referred to as a checklist or tally sheet of events. A data sample is used to determine the frequency of an event. The recording of data, survey, or sample objectively validates the significance of the event. This usually follows the Pareto analysis or cause-and-effect diagram to verify a problem or cause. This tool is often used to establish a frequency or histogram chart.

The check sheet is created by doing the following:

1. Clarifying what must be collected objectively.
2. Establishing the format for the data collection. (It should be easily understood by the collector. Everyone involved should also understand the objective of collection to ensure accuracy of the collection process.)
3. Establishing the sample size and time frame of data collection.
4. For consistency, training data collectors.
5. Observing, recording, and collecting data.
6. Tallying results using Pareto charts or histograms.
7. Evaluating results. Evaluation by the team process provides optimal understanding and verification of data collected.

Using a check sheet provides objective factual data to evaluate problems or causes early in the problem-solving process. This tracking method detects patterns that occur in the process and provides data for Pareto charts or histograms. The advantages of this tool are that it defines areas to discuss, limits the scope of an investigation, is an organized approach, and documents results. However, it is possible to over-rely on check sheets. Those preparing a check sheet should strive to avoid bias, mix questions by topic, test questions prior to use, and allow for "I don't know" as a reply. Suggestions for using a checklist include the following:

- To learn the reason questions are asked.
- To determine applicability of the completeness of the questions.

Exhibit A-2. Sample Check Sheet Form

ABENDS (Daily System)	February 24–28, 1994					
	Day 1	Day 2	Day 3	Day 4	Day 5	Total

- To rehearse questions.
- To anticipate responses.
- To ask questions without using a questionnaire.
- To document answers when an interview is complete.

Exhibit A-2 shows a sample check sheet form.

CONTROL CHARTS

Control charts are the result of a statistical technique to assess, monitor, and document the stability of a process. They can be used to monitor a continuous repeatable process and the process's variation from specifications. Control charts monitor the variation of a statistically stable process with activities. Two types of variation are observed: common, or random, events and special, or unique, events. Control charts evaluate variations in a process to determine what improvements are needed. They should be used continually to monitor processes.

A decision to use control charts should not be taken lightly. Normally, it is taken when a process is thought to be out of control. Initially, a team evaluates what is going wrong by using brainstorming, Pareto analysis, and cause-and-effect diagrams to understand the problem. The steps to create a control chart include the following:

1. Identify characteristics of process to monitor — defects, cycle times, abends, cost, or maintenance.
2. Select the appropriate type of control chart based on characteristics to monitor.
3. Determine methods for sampling (how many, over what time frame), use check sheets.
4. Collect sample data.

Analyze and calculate sample statistics: average, standard deviation, upper limit, lower limit.

Construct a control chart based on statistics.

Monitor process for common and special causes.

A process is in control when observations fall within limits. The causes of any observation outside the limits must be analyzed.

It is important to investigate unusual patterns when observations have multiple runs above or below average. A process shift is occurring and needs to be understood. This may lead to process improvements or corrections.

A control chart objectively defines a process and variation, establishes measures for a process, and improves process analysis and opportunities. Process improvements are based on facts and managed by facts. Control charts can be used to monitor anything that can be measured.

Exhibit A-3 illustrates two control charts that measure software maintenance costs.

HISTOGRAMS

A histogram, or frequency distribution chart, is a bar graph of measured values that displays the frequency of occurrences of its measured data. It is an orderly technique of grouping data by predetermined intervals to show their frequency. It provides a way to measure and analyze data collected about a process or problem. Pareto charts are a special use of a histogram. When sufficient data on a process is available, a histogram displays the process central point or average, variation or standard deviation and shape of distribution (e.g., normal, skewed, clustered). Exhibit A-4 illustrates a simple histogram.

Creating a histogram requires some understanding of the data set being measured. To gain it, the following steps should be taken:

1. Gather data and organize from lowest to highest values.
2. Calculate the range (r): largest less smallest.

	Project 1	Project 2	Project 3	Project 4
January	$1000	$2000	$2000	$3000
February	2000	1000	3000	6000
March	1000	2000	3000	9000
April	2000	3000	2000	4000
May	1000	1000	2000	7000
June	2000	1000	1000	5000
Total	$9000	$10,000	$13,000	$34,000

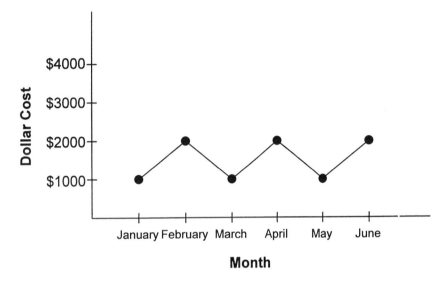

Exhibit A-3. Software Maintenance Control Charts

3. Determine number of cells (k): usually between 7 and 13.
4. Calculate the interval or width (m) of the cells:

$$m = \frac{\text{range}}{K}$$

5. Sort the data or observations into their respective cells.
6. Count the data points of each cell (i.e., frequency) to determine the height of the interval. Create a frequency table.
7. Plot the results by drawing bars.

A histogram helps explain graphically if a process is in control, provides a basis for what to work on first (especially by using the Pareto chart application), provides insight on a process's capability to meet customer specifications, and establishes a technique to measure a process. It can also help analyze opportunities for improvement. Teams should use a histogram technique if they want to understand the nature of the processes they are accountable for or own.

Interval	Tabulation	Cumulative Frequency	Frequency
0-3	11	2	2
3-6	1111 1	6	8
6-9	111	3	11

Bar Chart:

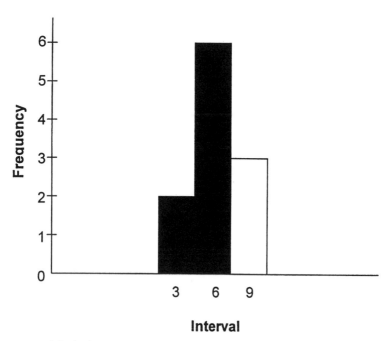

Interval

Variation:
1. Polygon: Draw line from midpoints of bars.
2. Add range of acceptable values (e.g., within plus/minus 5 of budget) to show if actual values lie within acceptable range.

Exhibit A-4. Sample Histogram

RUN CHARTS

A run chart is a graph of data in chronological order that displays shifts in a central tendency. Run charts track changes or trends in a process, as well as help users understand the process dynamics. This technique is often used before a control chart is developed to monitor a process. A run chart is established for measuring events or observations in a time or sequence order (see Exhibit A-5).

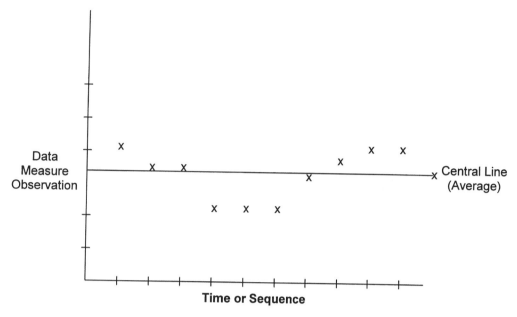

Exhibit A-5. Sample Run Chart

A run chart is created by following these steps:

1. Decide which outputs of a process to measure.
2. Label the chart vertically (for quantity) and horizontally (for time).
3. Plot the individual measurements over time (once per time interval, or as they become available).
4. Connect data points for easy use and interpretation.

Data must be tracked chronologically. Key interpretation of certain patterns when monitoring the data points include the following:

- *Unusual events.* Eight or more data points above or below the average value indicates the average has changed and must be investigated. If the shift is favorable, it should be made a permanent part of the process. If unfavorable, it should be eliminated.
- *Trend.* Six or more data points of continuous increase or decrease. Neither pattern would be expected to happen based on random chance. It strongly indicates that an important change has occurred and needs to be investigated.
- *Two processes.* Fourteen or more data points in a row alternating up or down indicates two distinct patterns caused by two groups, two shifts, or two people.
- *Special causes.* These need to be investigated to determine these patterns.

A run chart monitors process outputs, provides a means to detect process trends, and provides input for establishing control charts after a process has matured or stabilized in time. Run charts can monitor complaint levels, customer satisfaction levels, suggestion levels, training efforts, number of invoices, number of system errors, and downtime. Several samples of run charts can be used to begin to build a control chart.

SCATTER PLOTS OR DIAGRAMS

A scatter plot or diagram shows the relationship that might exist between two variables. It can test for possible cause-and-effect relationships. Often referred to as correlation diagrams, scatter plots explore possible relationships between a variable and a response to test how one variable influences the response. Typical scatter diagrams are illustrated in Exhibit A-6.

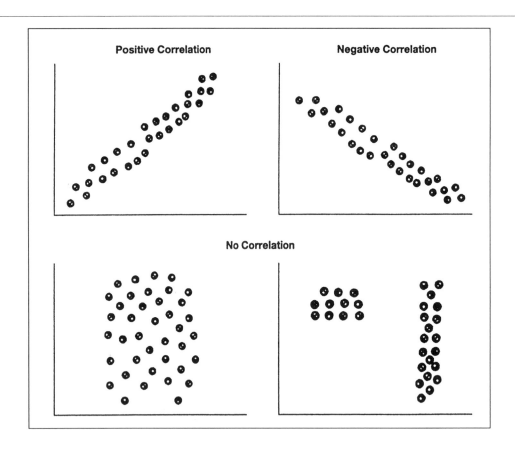

Exhibit A-6. Typical Scatter Diagrams

A scatter plot can be created by following these steps:

1. Select the variable and response relationship to be examined by the team.
2. Gather data on variable and response; determine sample size of paired data.
3. Plot the result; determine appropriate scale to plot the relationship.

Repeated data points should be circled as many times as they occur. The pattern of the plots reveals any correlation—positive, negative, random, linear, curvilinear, or cluster. A frequent error in interpreting results is assuming that no relationship exists between a variable and a response because a relationship is not immediately apparent. Another sample may be necessary in such cases.

A scatter plot provides analysis between two measurement variables in a process, provides a test of two variables being changed to improve a process or solve a problem, or helps to uncover real causes, not symptoms, of a problem or process. Examples of scatter plots include the following:

- Defect level versus complexity.
- Defects versus skill levels.
- Failures versus time.
- Cost versus time.
- Change response versus personnel availability.
- Defect cost versus lifecycle.
- Preventive cost versus failure cost.

Exhibits A-7, A-8, and A-9 are some sample scatter plots.

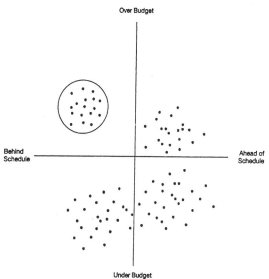

Exhibit A-7. Cluster Analysis Using a Scatter Plot

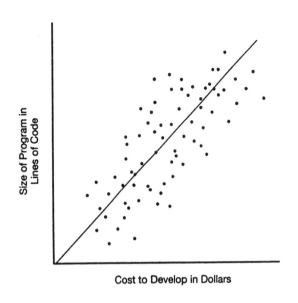

Exhibit A-8. Regression Analysis Using a Scatter Plot

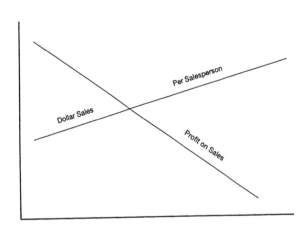

Exhibit A-9. Multivariate Analysis

Appendix B
Team Tools:
Affinity Diagrams

A group takes the verbal data (i.e., ideas, opinions, and issues) developed in brainstorming and separates them into categories to create an affinity diagram. Teams use affinity diagrams to help create order out of chaos and to understand and teach one another. This technique can do the following:

- Help define a problem.
- Expose obscure problems.
- Organize fuzzy ideas.
- Provide direction to take in problem solving.
- Categorize and simplify brainstorming results.

Team members follow these steps:

1. Write ideas, opinions, or issues on index cards or adhesive notes. (This can be done during the brainstorm session, as well.)
2. Randomly place written forms on a flat surface, wallboard, or flipchart.
3. Instruct team members to place written forms into meaningful groups — similar, related, or common.
4. Allow step three to continue until five or fewer groupings result.
5. Have team members label or agree on the best description of each resulting group.
6. Document the results into a listing of related groups or an affinity diagram.

Affinity diagrams can be used to discover why policies do not exist, why standards are not adhered to, why Total Quality Management (TQM) or quality assurance (QA) failed, and why objective measures are not used to understand the leadership role in TQM. They can also be used to find out why employees are not involved, to find out why quality does not work, or to improve teamwork in the workplace. They can help define the team processes, establish measures, and rank improvement opportunities.

BENCHMARKING

Benchmarking determines organizational performance relative to other organizations (both competitors and noncompetitors). The objective is to understand the competitors' capabilities, compare them with best practices, establish goals, and develop true measures of productivity. By studying others, a team can better understand its processes and practices. Usually, management and project leaders work closely with marketing and technical personnel in developing a benchmarking process.

Implementing a benchmark process is not easy. An information services organization should work with other organizations, such as marketing, to establish this process. To conduct benchmarking or implement a process, a team should take the following steps:

1. Select what to benchmark. Customer data on expectations is a source of what to benchmark.
2. Determine the potential impact or value for comparative data.
3. Determine who are the best in class, and who has similar processes, similar requirements, or a similar-sized organization.
4. Determine the data needed, collection method, and data analysis procedures.
5. Determine the source of data — interviews, questionnaires, surveys, consultants, journals, trade publications, advertisements, and annual reports.
6. Join forum groups or consortiums.
7. Assess performance gaps between the process, products, or services being benchmarked.
8. Communicate findings with team members and interrelated groups.
9. Establish improvement goals.
10. Develop, implement, and monitor action plans.
11. Periodically reexamine benchmark data sources for validity and changes.

Benchmarking provides insight on how well an organization meets its customers' needs compared with how well its competitors do. It also provides a way to compare the organization's performance with the best in its class. Benchmarking can be used to compare the following:

- Outsourcing versus in-house services.
- The value of products or services.
- Defect rates.
- Cycle times.
- Complaints and follow-up.
- Customer satisfaction levels.
- Employee satisfaction levels.

BRAINSTORMING

This technique is a powerful way to explore creative options, especially for a team to get started in understanding what is happening with a process or problem. The approach allows all team members to contribute equally. In a brainstorming session, ideas are generated fast, then carefully reviewed. The team weeds out ideas for duplication, nonessentials, unworkable, and unrelated ideas.

Some methods used for brainstorming are as follows:

- *Round table.* Team members take turns sharing ideas. The session ends when everyone has expressed his or her ideas.
- *Note card.* A structured technique for team members to record their ideas. Each writes down his or her ideas on note cards. Ideas are posted for all team members to view. This provides an anonymous process for large groups to express their ideas.
- *Free form.* This spontaneous method captures fast-paced ideas freely flowing from a team. It requires fast recording and ends when ideas are exhausted. A creative process open to wild ideas, less-assertive team members can be drowned out.

Brainstorming can be used to do the following:

- Review existing processes (e.g., inputs, outputs, and flows).
- Resequence existing processes.
- Eliminate wasteful and redundant work activities.
- Reengineer a process, product, or service.
- Design a new or improved process.
- Establish standards, guidelines, or measures.

Brainstorming is a prerequisite for using other tools, such as an affinity diagram, Pareto analysis, or a cause-and-effect diagram.

The brainstorming tool requires a method to capture all pertinent information. Each member needs to actively participate and be willing to share ideas, opinions, concerns, issues, and experiences. At the beginning, the facilitator needs to establish basic ground rules and a code of conduct. The following steps can be used to conduct a brainstorm session:

1. Agree on what is being brainstormed.
2. Agree on a structured or unstructured approach.
3. Record all ideas.
4. Make the session short (e.g., 5 to 15 minutes).
5. Stop the session when ideas become redundant or infrequent.
6. Have team members review their ideas for redundancy and clarification, eliminating ideas when necessary.

Brainstorming can be used to create a list of ideas to evaluate, a starting point for solving problems, or a clearer understanding of problems or causes. It is an easy tool for generating creative or original ideas about a process, problem, product, or service. Brainstorming rules should include the following principles:

- All members have an equal opportunity to participate.
- No criticism is allowed.
- No idea should be treated as insignificant.
- No rank should be observed.
- One conversation is allowed at a time.
- A free-wheeling environment is encouraged.
- Participants should think creatively.
- Participants should express the problem in a simple and complete sentence.
- All ideas should be recorded in a manner visible to the entire group.

NOMINAL GROUP TECHNIQUE

This structured brainstorming technique allows team members equal opportunity in ranking their ideas, issues, or concerns. In brainstorming, depending on the team makeup or the situation being brainstormed, a structured approach is effective. Nominal grouping uses a round table or written card method to allow equal participation of team members. A good technique to gather large amounts of information, this approach is designed to rank ideas.

The steps for this technique vary, depending on the question or situation and the number of responses from the brainstorm process. This technique should be practiced only by a trained facilitator. It should include the following steps:

1. The problem or topic must be clearly stated in writing for the team or group.
2. A round-table or written note card method should be used.
3. All members should be allowed to share their ideas.
4. All input should be recorded. Redundant or similar ideas should be merged if the group agrees to do so.
5. After all inputs are recorded, a list should be provided. If there are large amounts of input, a Pareto technique should be used to reduce the list to a manageable few. Votes received by each input should be added, sorted high to low, and the 10 highest vote-getters should be taken. In case of ties for 10th place, all tied inputs should be taken.
6. Remaining inputs should be listed (labeled alphabetically or numerically), and participants should rank them by importance.

The nominal group technique can be used to reach consensus on such matters as

- Which defect is the greatest?
- Who are the organization's customers?
- What are the organization's impediments to quality improvement?
- What new standards are needed?
- What are the key indicators?
- What tool is not being used effectively and how can its usage be increased?
- How can the organization get a quality tool used?

Workpaper B-1 can be used when practicing the nominal group technique.

FLOWCHARTS

An effective diagram that displays the sequential steps of an event, process, or workflow, flowcharts are sometimes referred to as process mapping. The flowchart technique should be standard for any information services function. Every information technology (IT) professional needs to develop skills to create a flowchart and know where to apply the tool. The application is most useful when applied by a team to understand a process to improve it. Teams often use this technique to obtain a common vision of what a process should do or look like. Exhibit B-1 is a sample flowchart.

Flowcharts may be used to describe several types of processes.

A stable or known process is operational. It is monitored for common and special causes. Special causes need to be evaluated to determine where the

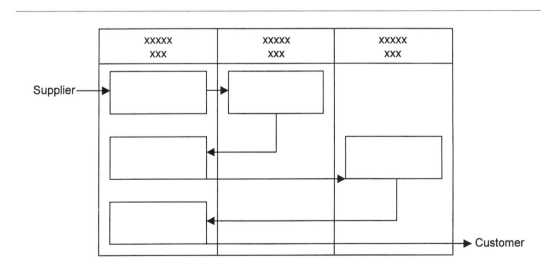

Exhibit B-1. Sample Flowchart for Defining a Process

Workpaper B-1. Brainstorming Item List

Item	Rank

unusual situation or element occurred in the process. A process cause-and-effect diagram is helpful in examining special causes and evaluating weak points.

If a process needs a deliberate change to stabilize it, teams can use several tools with a flowchart—brainstorming, an affinity diagram, and a cause-and-effect diagram—to determine the impact of change. The force field analysis helps remove obstacles working against change.

With new or unknown processes, teams can create a flowchart of the planned or optimal process.

To construct a flowchart, a team must do the following:

1. Identify the major function or activity being performed or needed to be performed.
2. Identify tasks to support the function or activity.
3. Determine the steps needed to do the tasks.
4. Sequence the activity, tasks, and steps.
5. Connect the activity, tasks, and steps using directional arrows or connections.
6. Research consensus on the process as viewed from a flowchart.

Creating a flow chart is a structured technique that orders the sequential steps of a process visually. It can be used to highlight inefficiency or redundancy in a process.

FORCE FIELD ANALYSIS

Force field analysis is a team tool to determine the forces that drive and restrain a change process. This technique gets team members to understand all facets of a desired change by using creative thinking. This approach is effective in leading members to agree about the relative priority of factors on these forces. Recognizing the barriers to change can facilitate reaching this consensus.

The process begins when the team defines the existing process and establishes improvements needed for changing it. At this point, the team should do the following:

1. Establish a desired situation or goal statement.
2. Brainstorm about all possible forces driving or restraining this goal.
3. List separately driving and restraining forces.
4. Determine relative importance and reach consensus on these forces.
5. Create a force field diagram (see Exhibit B-2).
6. Select the most significant forces that need to be acted on. Diminish the restraining or strengthening driving forces by using the nominal group technique.

Driving Forces	Restraining Forces

Quality Focus ⟶

Common Goals ⟶ ⟵ Time Commitment

Change Reward Process ⟶ ⟵ Knowledge

Teamwork ⟶ ⟵ Culture Existing

Results ⟶ ⟵ Fear (i.e., loss of job)

Training ⟶ ⟵ Change

Customer Feedback ⟶ ⟵ Cost

Customer Involvement ⟶ ⟵ Priority

Commitment ⟶ ⟵ Limited Resources

Experience (in other areas) ⟶ ⟵ Failures

Successes ⟶ ⟵ Risk

⟵ Reviews

Exhibit B-2. Sample Force Field Analysis for Need Management Involvement in Quality Leadership Process

The team then proceeds to a plan of action based on the forces selected in the last step. Force field analysis can be used to implement quality assurance functions, implement IT, develop education and training programs, establish a measurement program, select a new technique or tool for conducting meaningful meetings, and empower a work force.

MATRIX DATA ANALYSIS

A matrix technique can be used to show the relationship between any two measurable characteristics. This technique is also referred to as matrix check-sheet or matrix diagrams. Matrix data analysis is frequently used to identify whether customer needs are being met, have changed, or no longer exist. This approach can also support the determination of system requirements. In particular, teams use it when they need to understand and analyze customer preferences. This tool helps teams view a problem as a whole for clarity, especially when it is used with the joint application design process.

For multidimensional problems, this approach focuses on the essential factors in problem areas. The matrix data analysis allows a team to test, evaluate, and develop strategies.

Use of this tool requires an understanding and use of matrices and the T-type matrix structure. To produce a T-type matrix, the following steps can be used:

1. Format or organize a matrix diagram.
2. Sort the phenomenon, or problems, by subject matter.
3. Sort the causes related to the problem.
4. List the processes or procedures as they are performed.
5. Determine the relationship among problems and causes (i.e., strong, probable, or none).
6. Determine the relationship between causes and processes (i.e., strong, probable, or none).
7. Recheck the relationships for validation and verification. A team needs to reach consensus on these relationships.
8. Evaluate and score the importance of relationships: strong = 3; probable = 2; and none = 1.

The matrix diagram method helps teams sort verbal information for discussion; focus should be kept on what is important and on clarifying the strength of relationships. Matrix data analysis can be used to do the following:

- Identify customer needs satisfaction.
- Understand a problem.
- Structure the problem-solving process.
- Establish a strategy for solving problems.
- Help define processes.
- Analyze process improvement opportunities.

Appendix C
Surveys and Interviews: What is a Structured Interview, and When Should It Be Used?

An essential part of teamwork is collecting data from individuals. The two most common methods to do this are surveys and interviews. There are advantages to both. However, it is important that surveys and interviews be performed in a structured manner.

This appendix describes the attributes of surveys and structured interviews. It explains the advantages of both. A structured interview tool is then described in depth.

A survey contains questions presented in a systematic, precise fashion. It enables the interviewer to obtain uniform data that can be compared, summed, and, if it is quantitative, subjected to additional statistical analysis. The form of a survey varies according to whether it is to be used in a structured interview, as a self-administered questionnaire (either mailed to individuals or organizations or completed by individuals in a group setting), or as a pro forma schedule to obtain information from records.

An interview that uses a survey to gather data—either by telephone or face to face—is a structured interview. Evaluators ask in a precise manner the same questions of numerous individuals or individuals who represent numerous organizations, offering each interviewee the same set of possible responses. In contrast, an unstructured interview contains many open-ended questions that are not asked in a structured, precise manner. Different interviewers interpret questions and often offer different explanations when asked for clarification.

Given the need to collect uniform data from numerous persons or organizations, when should an interviewer use a structured interview rather than a mail survey or a survey administered in a group setting? There is no hard and fast answer. Some of the advantages and disadvantages of interviews

Exhibit C-1. Comparison of Survey Techniques

	Extent of advantage				
	Structure interview		Questionnaire		
Characteristic or advantage	**By telephone**	**Face to face**	**By mail**	**Group**	**Audit of records**
Methodology					
Allows use of probes	3	5	1	2	n/a
Controls bias of collector	3	2	5	4	5
Can overcome unexpected events	4	5	2	3	4
Facilitates feedback	4	5	2	5	2
Allows oral and visual inquiry	1	5	2	5	n/a
Allows oral and visual response	1	5	2	2	2
Evaluator can control survey procedures	3	5	1	4	5
Facilitates interchange with source	4	5	2	5	n/a
What contents allow					
Inclusion of most relevant variables	3	5	4	4	3
Complex subject matter to be presented or derived	3	5	3	4	4
Collection of real-time data	5	5	4	5	3
Acquisition of historical data	4	4	4	4	5
Universe or sample					
Relevant universe to be sampled can be identified	4	5	4	5	4
Facilitates contacting and getting sample	3	2	4	4	5
Allows use with large sample	4	3	5	4	5
Allows identity of source to be known	4	5	3	5	3
Reduces problems from respondent's illiteracy	4	5	1	3	n/a
What time, cost, and resources minimize					
Instrument-development time	2	3	1	1	5

Exhibit C-1. Comparison of Survey Techniques *(Continued)*

	Extent of advantage				
	Structure interview		Questionnaire		
Characteristic or advantage	**By telephone**	**Face to face**	**By mail**	**Group**	**Audit of records**
Instrument-development cost	3	1	1	1	5
Number of field staff	5	?	5	?	?
Travel by staff	5	?	5	?	?
Staff training	2	1	5	3	5
Time required to carry out activities	?	?	3	?	?
Overall cost	3	1	5	4	1
Results, response, and quality of data					
Maximize rate of return of data after source is contacted	4	5	3	5	n/a
Minimize multiple contacts of sources	2	2	3	4	n/a
Minimize follow-up after initial response	5	5	3	4	5
Increase chance source will be accurate	4	4	4	4	3
Allow reliability to be checked	5	5	3	4	4
Allow validity to be checked	4	4	2	4	5
Facilitate recall of data by source	4	5	3	4	n/a
Notes: 1 Little or no extent 　　　5 Very great extent 2 Some extent 　　　? Depends greatly upon study specification 3 Moderate extent 　　n/a Not applicable 4 Great extent					

and surveys are discussed in the following paragraphs. In addition, the characteristics of various data-collection techniques are systematically compared in Exhibit C-1.

An interview is often more effective in the design phase of an evaluation. Face-to-face interviews and telephone interviews are generally more successful when respondents have low reading levels and the questions are complex.

Telephone interviews and face-to-face interviews enable an interviewer to establish rapport with the respondents. Individuals who would ignore mail questionnaires or who would not answer certain questions on them can be persuaded to provide truthful answers in a telephone or face-to-face interview. In addition, a well-trained interviewer can recognize when a respondent is having a problem understanding or interpreting a question and can use the proper techniques to assist the interviewee without jeopardizing the integrity of the interview.

Compared with a telephone interview, a face-to-face interview gives the interviewer the opportunity to observe as well as listen. In addition, more complex questions can be asked during a face-to-face interview than in a telephone interview. Respondents can be shown cards with the complete set of possible responses, making it easier for them to remember and consider all the choices. In addition, more questions can be asked. Twenty to 30 minutes is the usual limit for telephone interviews, but face-to-face interviews can last up to an hour.

Computer-assisted telephone interviewing (CATI) is one form of telephone interviewing. Wish CATI, the survey is stored in a computer, questions are displayed on a computer screen during the interview, and the interviewer directly enters the responses into the computer. Telephone interviews cost more than mail surveys but less than personal interviews. Depending on the size of the sample, the number of interviewers available, the number of questions, and question complexity, telephone surveys can also be completed quickly.

Compared with a mail survey, face-to-face and telephone interviews are much faster methods of gathering data. The need to train interviewers and their time spent traveling and contacting and interviewing respondents, however, makes face-to-face interviews much more expensive than telephone interviews or mail or group surveys. Both forms of surveys can be longer and can include more complex questions (if the respondent group reads well) than is possible with a telephone interview.

To administer a survey in a group setting, it must be practical to assemble the respondents. Thus, it is normally used in situations in which the sample is an entire group or a large portion of it, such as an army company or battalion or all or many agency employees in one location. Group surveys are faster than mail surveys and permit some clarification of questions (but not to the same extent as interviews).

DESIGNING A STRUCTURED INTERVIEW

Designing a structured interview requires more than just writing down a set of questions to be asked. This section examines the process by which the interview questions are identified, developed, and selected. It then describes standard procedures for composing and formatting the questions. These procedures aim to ensure that the data collected is reliable and valid and to facilitate trouble-free editing and analysis of data, while keeping the burden on the interviewee to a minimum.

In some organizations, management designates representatives and establishes procedures that must be followed when using structured interviews and questionnaires.

IDENTIFYING VARIABLES AND DEVELOPING QUESTIONS

The first step is to formulate the broad, overall questions to be answered by the evaluation or audit. Why is the study being done? Is it designed to describe what has taken place in a program or to compare what has happened with some established or implied standard, a normative question, or if a program has made a difference, a cause-and-effect question? Examples of such questions are as follows:

- *Descriptive.* "How do graduates of the XYZ program for the unemployed seek out and find jobs in the community?"
- *Normative.* "How well does the program meet its goals for placing graduates in jobs?"
- *Cause-and-effect.* "Why do some graduates find jobs and others do not find jobs?"

The type of question asked dictates the evaluation strategy, and certain strategies are more appropriate to answering certain questions. However, structured interviews can be used with several evaluation strategies and, thus, in a variety of assignments.

After the broad overall questions are developed, they must be translated into measurable elements in the form of hypotheses or questions. For the previous example, evaluating how participants found jobs requires developing such measures as the sources through which participants learned of available jobs, the number of employers contacted, and the number of job interviews arranged. Next, the target population must be identified. The target population is the source level (individuals, groups, or organizations) at which the information is to be gathered. Thus, in the study of how program participants found jobs after leaving the program, the target population is the individual participants of the program who were trained.

The next step is to develop a pool of questions that attempt to measure the variables under consideration. The questions may include various ways of measuring the same variable. For example, for age, an interviewer might ask, "How old were you on your last birthday?" or "On what day, month, and year were you born?" Both questions help determine an individual's age, but the second elicits much more information. From the pool of questions, then, the most useful or appropriate are chosen. Exhibit C-2 illustrates the process of identifying, developing, and selecting questions for a study of how program participants found jobs after leaving a job-training program.

COMPOSING APPROPRIATE QUESTIONS

Interview questions must be appropriate, that is, relevant to the study, directed to the proper persons, and easily answered. Questions should be relevant to the study being conducted and should have a good probability of yielding data needed for the final report. Although this seems obvious, interviewers sometimes go on fishing expeditions and want to include all sorts of variables that can create an unnecessary burden on the interviewee and distract attention from the central purpose of the interview.

Preliminary consideration should be given to which people can be expected to answer given questions. A question may be relevant to a given study, but the choice of persons to answer it may be inappropriate.

Interviews are meant to obtain data that may otherwise not be documented or, if documented, may need some interpretation. This includes opinions and feelings about the study topic. Questions should be relatively easy to answer and should not cause undue burden to an interviewee.

It is wise to avoid questions that require an interviewee to research the issue before answering. If used at all, such questions should be reserved for mail questionnaires. For telephone interviews, questions should be even less complex, because there is less of an opportunity to help an interviewee understand them. It is possible to send the questionnaire beforehand to the person who will be interviewed, requesting that he or she gather the necessary information in preparation for the interview.

Other questions (or the manner in which they are presented) that cause an interviewee discomfort should be avoided or used with extreme care. The same is true of questions that would tend to incriminate or show an interviewee in a bad light, particularly because the person might end the interview if the questions are asked. Likewise, it is best to avoid personal questions about private matters that are not appropriate to the study, as well as questions whose sole purpose is to embarrass the interviewee (such as testing or questioning the intelligence of the interviewee or seeking information about private habits).

Exhibit C-2. Identifying, Developing, and Selecting Questions

Task	Example
Formulate overall questions	How do program participants find jobs after leaving the XYZ program?
Determine the kind of information needed	1. Sources through which participants learned of available jobs 2. Number of employers contacted 3. Number of job interviews arranged 4. Number of interviews attended 5. Number of jobs offered 6. Time (in days) it took to secure a job 7. Time (in days) since participant left program to date of survey 8. Relationship of job obtained to skill...
Identify target population	Program participants who have left the program (random sample)

Create a question pool	1.1 How did you look for jobs?
	    1. Look in the newspaper?
	    2. Ask friends?
	    3. Go to a state employment office?
	    4. Go to a private employment office?
	    5. Look in the telephone book?
	    6. Drop in on companies?
	    7. Get information from radio or TV?
	1.2 About how many jobs that you were interested in did you find out about from
	    1. The newspaper?
	    2. A friend?
	    3. The state employment service?
	    4. Private employment services?
	2.1 How many employers did you contact about a job since you left the program?
	2.2 Since you left the program, about how many employers did you contact about a job that you heard from
	    1. The newspaper?
	    2. A friend?
	    3. The state employment service?
	3.1 How many...

Select questions	1.1... 2.1... 3.1...

If needed, sensitive questions can be asked in a mail questionnaire, where confidentiality or anonymity can be granted. It is also wise to avoid questions that could cause unnecessary confrontation, causing the interviewer and interviewee to take sides and do battle. This detracts from the interview task, may cause bias, and can seriously affect the validity of the answers given.

It is also important to avoid questions that have no answers and questions that produce unusable results. These are not to be confused, of course, with questions for which the legitimate answer might be "no basis to judge" or "no opinion" (presumably, some interviewees will not have a basis to make a judgment or give an opinion).

SELECTING A QUESTION FORMAT

When deciding on the format or type of question to use, the interviewer should consider how the question is delivered or presented, what the interviewee is asked, and available response alternatives. The types of questions that can be used include open-ended, fill-in-the-blank, yes or no, and scaled-response, as discussed in the following sections.

Open-Ended Questions

An open-ended question provides no structure for an answer, allowing the interviewee to discuss what he or she wishes, not necessarily what the interviewer wants to know. By sharpening the question, the questioner can focus it. Some examples follow:

- *Broad question.* "What happened to you while you were unemployed?"
- *Focused question.* "How did you manage to pay your bills while you were unemployed?"

Open-ended questions are easy to write. For initial research, they can be used successfully to elicit answers that contribute to the formulation of specific questions and response alternatives. For a small number of respondents and where analysis may be qualitative rather than quantitative open-ended questions may also be useful. If possible, it is best to avoid using open-ended questions with large numbers of respondents, whose answers need to be tabulated. Under such circumstances, content analysis should be done before attempting to tabulate.

The questions for CATIs should be designed in accordance with the guidelines established for structured telephone surveys. Other practices may also apply. For example, open-ended questions should be avoided as much as possible, primarily because of the time it takes to type the answer. If the topics addressed in the questionnaire are at the exploratory stage, a CATI is not recommended. A CATI requires the respondents to understand the issues being investigated. To the extent that open-ended questions are included in a CATI, they should be designed for quick anwers. Such questions take up considerable space in the computer data files. To the extent possible, they should be moved to the end of the questionnaire and the interviewer should attempt to record the answers offline. These questions have the potential for interrupting the flow of the CATI and deflating the interview.

A question that actually is closed can be presented in such a way that it appears to be open-ended to the interviewee. This is done by preparing a list of potential answers and checking these off during the interview, as the interviewee mentions the various alternatives. It is important, however, to read the choices to the interviewee. Such questions are more focused and specific than simple, open-ended questions and allow the range of possible answers to be narrowed.

Fill-in-the-Blank Questions

This type of question has a simple answer, usually in the form of a name, frequency, or amount. Interviewers can prepare a list of alternative answers to check off during the interview.

Yes-No Questions

This is the most typical type of question. It is a good format for obtaining factual information but generally not opinions or feelings. Because the interviewee is asked to make a commitment to one extreme or another, his or her choice is considered forced.

Scaled-Response Questions

In a scaled-response question, the interviewer shows an interviewee a scale — a list of alternative responses that increase or decrease in intensity in an ordered fashion. There are three types: balanced, unbalanced, and rating and ranking scales.

Balanced Scales. The end points of a balanced scale are usually adjectives or phrases with opposite meanings, for example, very satisfied and very dissatisfied. As its name implies, a balanced-scale survey contains an equal number of responses on each side of a reference point or neutral response (see Exhibit C-3). This scale expands the yes-no answer, permitting a range of answers that better reflect the way people hold opinions.

Unbalanced Scales. Interviewers use an unbalanced scale when no negative response is possible. It has a reference point (usually a "zero" point or "none"), and the value of the attribute increases for successive points on the scale. Intensity ranges from none to very great (see Exhibit C-4).

Rating and Ranking Scales. In a rating question, an interviewee is asked to assign a rating to persons, places, or things according to specified criteria.

Exhibit C-3. Sample Balanced Scale Question

How satisfied or dissatisfied are you with the typing ability of the secretaries in your division? *(Check one.)*
1. ☐ Very satisfied 2. ☐ Generally satisfied 3. ☐ Neither satisfied nor dissatisfied 4. ☐ Generally dissatisfied 5. ☐ Very dissatisfied

Exhibit C-4. Sample Unbalanced Scale Question

On your last assignment, how much opportunity, if any, were you given to help develop staff working for you? *(Check one.)*
1. ☐ Very great opportunity 2. ☐ Great opportunity 3. ☐ Moderate opportunity 4. ☐ Some opportunity 5. ☐ Little or no opportunity

Exhibit C-5. Sample Rating Question

Using the rating scale, rate each of the individuals listed below on their ability to do Band I Evaluator work. *(Check one for each person.)*

Staff	Exceptional	Superior	Fully successful	Borderline	Unacceptable
Smith					
Jones					
Anderson					
Columbus					
Michael					

The points on the scale can be either numeric or verbal. An example of a verbal scale is shown in Exhibit C-5. Whether verbal or numerical, a rating scale implies that the distance from one point to the next is the same on all parts of the scale.

In a ranking question, an interviewee is asked to place items in order according to a specified criterion, as shown in Exhibit C-6. Ranking questions may have several types of instructions. The interviewer can ask the interviewee to rank them all, as in the example, or to select the first (best) and the last (worst), the top three, or some other combination. In contrast to rating, ranking does not imply that the distance between points is the

Exhibit C-6. Sample Ranking Question

	Rank the following individuals on their overall ability to do Band II Evaluator work. Use 1 for the best, 2 for the second best, 3 for third best, 4 for fourth, and 5 for the last. *(Enter number for each.)*
	Smith
	Jones
	Anderson
	Columbus
	Michael

same on all parts of the scale. For example, if Johnson, Green, and Smith were ranked one, two, and three, respectively, the interviewee may not necessarily think that the gap between Johnson's and Green's performance is the same as the gap between Green's and Smith's.

When it is necessary to obtain the interviewee's opinion as to the distance between items (for example, how much better or worse one evaluator is than others), a rating question should be used. Although a rating question may also produce an ordering, a respondent may well give two or more items the same rating. If the interviewee must choose between seven or fewer items but it does not matter how much better he or she believes one item is than the others, a ranking question is likely to give the proper information. When several items must be ordered, however, it will probably be easier for the interviewees to rate them than to rank them. It is difficult to judge the order of a large number of items and avoid ties between items, especially in interviews. A final order can be produced by averaging the ratings over all respondents.

Number of Cues. The number of cues for scaled-response questions depends on the type of interviewee and type of analysis expected. There is generally a physical limit to the number of cues to which an interviewee can react, probably around seven. Most companies use five-point scales. Respondents with a keen interest in the study can be expected to handle a great number of cues. The more points on the scale, the better the eventual analysis of the data because more cues provide a more sensitive measure and give the analyst greater flexibility in selecting ways to analyze the data.

An even number of cues used in a balanced scale generally eliminates a middle or neutral point on the scale and forces an interviewee to commit to a positive or negative feeling. The use of an odd-numbered scale permits a neutral answer and more closely approximates the range of opinions or feelings people can have.

When the possible responses do not include "no basis to judge," "can't recall," or "no opinion," an interviewee may feel forced to select an inaccurate answer. The point is that some people honestly may be unable to answer a question. If there is good reason to believe this is so for members of the respondent group, the interviewer should include in the list of cues read or shown to the interviewees the most applicable of the alternatives "no basis to judge," "can't recall," or "no opinion." If the interviewer does not do this, an interviewee may guess, make up an answer, or ignore the question.

Order of Cues. The order in which the cues are presented can help offset possible arguments that the interviewees are biased toward answering the question in a particular way. For example, if an organization had preliminary evidence that participants in a training program were not getting job counseling, the following question could be asked:

> Job counseling involves someone talking to you about how to apply for a job, how to behave in an interview, etc. To what extent did you receive job counseling while you were in this program?

The choices presented to the interviewee would be as follows:

- Very great extent.
- Great extent.
- Moderate extent.
- Some extent.
- Little or no extent.

In this example, the order of presentation biases the choice slightly in favor of the program. Some interviewees who did not take a strong interest in the question might select the first choice, indicating that they received job counseling to a very great extent. This would tend to give an overall answer that was slightly biased toward receiving job counseling.

When the cues form a scale, the bias inherent in the order in which the alternative responses are presented can be eliminated only at great expense.

To totally eliminate this type of bias, half the sample must receive the cues in one order and the other half must receive them in the opposite order. In the previous example, half the sample would be presented a card on which "very great extent" was the first (or top) cue and "little or no extent" was the last (or bottom) cue. The other half of the sample would be presented a card on which "little or no extent" was the first cue and "very great extent" was the last cue.

Wording of Cues. As indicated in the previous example, the scale used in the cues was the "extent" to which some action was performed. When an action or process is being assessed in a question, it is preferable to present the question and the cues in terms of the action. The previous question would generally be rephrased as "How much job counseling did you receive?" The cues could be rephrased as "A very great amount of counseling," "A great amount of counseling," "A moderate amount of counseling," and so on.

Unscaled-Response Questions

In an unscaled-response question, a list of cues is read or shown to the interviewee, who is asked to choose one from the list or to select all that apply. The list should consist of mutually exclusive categories. An "other" category is usually included as a last alternative, either to provide for many possible (but thought to be rare) answers or if it is thought that some interviewees will come up with unique answers. Exhibit C-7 is an example of a question in which only one response is to be given. Exhibit C-8 is a question in which the interviewee may check several responses.

ORGANIZING QUESTIONS

In any survey, the order in which the questions are presented is important. Early questions, which set the tone for the collection procedure and can influence responses to later questions, also help the interviewer get to know an interviewee and establish the rapport essential to a successful interview. For example, in an interview with participants in the XYZ program, the first few questions could review for accuracy data obtained from agency files, such as family composition, age, and education.

The next questions should also be answered with some ease. Should these early questions be too difficult or too sensitive for the level of relationship developed, an interviewee might end the interview. The questions should hold the interviewee's attention; thus, the interview must begin to

Exhibit C-7. Sample Unscaled Response Question with One Answer

Educationally, what is the highest level that you have achieved? *(Check one.)*
1. ☐ High school graduate 2. ☐ Some college 3. ☐ BS or BA degree 4. ☐ MS or MA degree 5. ☐ PhD 6. ☐ Other (specify) _____

Exhibit C-8. Sample Unscaled Response Question with Several Possible Answers

Please check the following possible eligibility requirements that you will be using to determine when you will offer remedial education to youths in your program. *(Check all that apply.)*
1. ☐ Scoring below a specific performance level on a READING test 2. ☐ Scoring below a specific performance level on a MATH test 3. ☐ Teacher recommendation 4. ☐ Youth or parent request 5. ☐ Youth must be a dropout 6. ☐ Age limits 7. ☐ Other (specify) _____

introduce some interesting questions and the sensitive areas covering the attitudes of the interviewee.

The questions should be presented logically. The interview should not haphazardly jump from one topic to another. The ordering of questions should not introduce bias. For example, to determine what the interviewee thinks a program's advantages and disadvantages are, the interviewer should not mention the possible advantages or disadvantages earlier in the interview.

Generally, the set of questions asked varies from interviewee to interviewee. Many questions are asked only if there is a specific response to a particular question. As a result, several questions may be skipped. These interrelationships among the questions constitute the skip pattern of the survey. For face-to-face interviews and telephone interviews that do not use a CATI system, the complexity of the survey's skip pattern should be kept to a minimum. Otherwise, it becomes very difficult for the interviewer to find the next question to be asked.

One of the important advantages of a CATI survey is that it allows for considerable complexity in the skip pattern because the computer handles the branching entirely. Any number of paths can be followed through the questionnaire. Usually, the computer displays the next question in sequence. Alternatively, conditional skips can be programmed to go from one specific question to another somewhat later in the questionnaire. These skips can be based on how the interviewee answers a single question or the responses to several questions.

One drawback to a CATI questionnaire is that multiple-choice questions that permit several answers are not easily handled. It is difficult for an interviewee to remember all the options when several can be chosen. As a result, multiple-choice questions that allow the interviewee to check all that apply (as illustrated in Exhibit C-8) should be broken down into separate questions, each of which is an alternative response that is "checked" or "not checked."

LAYOUT CONSIDERATIONS

The layout or form of a printed survey (for non-CATI applications) (see Exhibit C-9) is important; it is what the interviewer carries into the interview and uses as a guide to conduct it. It gives on-the-spot instructions for each question and allows the interviewer to record the answer. Later, the form is used to facilitate editing, keypunching, and the subsequent computerized analysis.

Here are some considerations when designing the survey:

- *Typeface.* Generally the text to be read to the interviewee is set off in a different typeface from the instructions that you do not read to the interviewee. In Exhibit C-9, for example, the text to be read to the interviewee is presented in uppercase and lowercase, and the instructions are in uppercase and lowercase italics.
- *Continuation of questions.* Generally, a question should not be continued in the next column or on the next page because the entire question or all the response alternatives may not be presented to the interviewee.
- *Boxes and lines.* Open-top boxes should be provided for the interviewer to record answers to questions that require written responses. The box or line should be placed in a standard place beside each question to aid the interviewer and to facilitate editing, data entry, and subsequent analysis of completed questionnaires.
- *Keypunch numbers.* These should be placed in a standard place beside each question to facilitate keypunching when data are entered into computer files.
- *Skipping questions.* If a certain response to a question means that interviewers are to skip the next question, specify this by placing a "go to" instruction beside the response.

APPROPRIATENESS OF THE LANGUAGE

What is said in the interview is basically dictated by the written, structured survey. It is prepared in advance and pretested, and the interviewers are trained to use it. Thus, to some extent, the appropriateness of the language has been tested. The interviewer must transmit faithfully to the interviewee the meaning of the questions. In addition to wording the questions precisely, it may be wise to include supplemental language in the survey, to be used if the interviewee does not understand the original wording of a question. If during the course of the interview the interviewee still does not understand and different language must be improvised, such improvisations should be noted and considered before the data are analyzed.

Exhibit C-9. Sample Structured Interview Text

Now I'd like to find out what you are doing.
1. Are you now receiving any AFDC? If yes, is this a full grant or reduced grant? *(Check one.)*
01. ☐ Yes—Full grant *(Go to Question 2)* 02. ☐ Yes—Reduced grant *(Go to Question 2)* 03. ☐ No *(Go to Question 3)*
2. What is your status with WIN? Are you registered in training or what? *(Listen, insert comments, and try to determine what code to assign. If necessary, check records or check with WIN staff afterwards. Check one.)*
01. ☐ Working registrant status 02. ☐ Part-time employment 03. ☐ Working nonregistrant 04. ☐ Institutional training 05. ☐ Work experience 06. ☐ WIN/OJT 07. ☐ WIN/PSE 08. ☐ Suspense to training 09. ☐ Suspense to employment 10. ☐ Intensive employability services 11. ☐ IES/Group job seeking activities 12. ☐ Other WIN noncomponent activity 13. ☐ Unassigned recipient
3. Are you looking for work (different work)? *(Check one.)*
1. ☐ Yes *(Go to Question 4)* 2. ☐ No *(Go to Question 5)*
4. How are you going about looking for work? *(Do not read choices; 1=mentioned; 2=not mentioned.)*
1. ☐ On my own 2. ☐ Through WIN 3. ☐ Through CETA 4. ☐ Through Employment Services (ES, SES) 5. ☐ Through private employment agency 6. Other *(Specify)* _____
5. To what extent are you having difficulty finding a job? *(Read choices; check one.)*
1. ☐ Very great extent *(Go to Question 6)* 2. ☐ Great extent *(Go to Question 6)* 3. ☐ Moderate extent *(Go to Question 6)* 4. ☐ Some extent *(Go to Question 6)* 5. ☐ Little or no extent *(Go to Question 9)*

The speech and mannerisms of the interviewer who controls the presentation of the interview questions and whose delivery of questions may alter their intended meaning is another important concern. More detailed information on this topic appears later in this appendix.

It is also important to consider the context of the interview in which each question is placed. Although, in designing the survey, it is wise to be precise about the order in which questions are asked, an interviewer may introduce some variation during the interview to clarify the questions, review information, or postpone potentially sensitive questions. Or if the interviewee expresses concern or sensitivity to a given question, changing the language of a subsequent question might defuse the concern.

LEVEL OF THE LANGUAGE

Those composing interview questions should consider the level of the language. They should seek to communicate at the level the interviewee understands and to create a verbal setting that is conducive to serious data gathering, yet one in which the interviewee is comfortable. One problem often encountered is maintaining a level of language that is neither above nor below the interviewee's level of understanding.

It is important not to speak over the interviewee's head by using complex, rare, and foreign words and expressions; words of many syllables; abbreviations; acronyms; and certain jargon. The interviewee may not understand such language, though it may seem appropriate to the interviewer or evaluation team.

Speaking over the interviewee's head hinders communication. Interviewees who are embarrassed at their lack of understanding may either not answer or guess at the meaning, which can lead to incorrect answers. Or the interviewee may get the impression that the interviewer does not care about the answer and lose interest in the interview.

Speaking down to an interviewee is just as bad. Oversimplifying the language in the survey can make interviewees feel that the interviewer regards them as ignorant. Likewise, care must be taken in using slang, folksy expressions, and certain jargon. Such language can help develop rapport with the interviewee, but the exactness of the communication may be lessened. Pretesting both the final wording of the survey and the interview approach helps avoid both problems.

USE OF QUALIFYING LANGUAGE

After composing an interview question, its author may find it requires an adjective or qualifying phrase added or a time specified to make the item complete or give the interviewee sufficient or complete information. For example, "How many employees do you have?" might become "How many full-time-equivalent employees do you have?" and "How many times have you gone to a physician?" might become "How many times have you gone to a physician in the past six months?"

If feedback is possible in the interview, the interviewee can ask for further qualification as needed. If the questions do not include the necessary qualifiers in the survey, however, another interviewer may qualify in a different way. This could make the resulting data difficult to summarize and analyze. In addition, interviewees, not realizing that qualifying language is absent, may answer the question as they interpret it. Thus, different interviewees would be responding to different questions based on their own interpretations.

CLARITY OF THE LANGUAGE

The style in which a question is couched can affect how well it communicates.

Length, Complexity, and Clutter

A question that contains too many ideas or concepts may be too complex for the interviewee to understand. This is especially true if the question is presented orally, which makes it difficult for the interviewee to review parts of the question. While the interviewee might respond to one part of the question, the interviewer may interpret the response as a response to the entire question. Each sentence should contain one thought, and the interviewee must be given the proper framework to interpret questions. For example, "How satisfied or dissatisfied were you with the amount of time devoted to helping you get a job while you were in the XYZ program?" becomes "Think about the training experiences you had while in the XYZ program. How satisfied or dissatisfied were you with the amount of time devoted to helping you get a job?"

Likewise, a sentence may contain words that clutter the message. Questions should be worded concisely. Here are a few tricks to reduce sentence clutter:

- Delete "that" wherever possible — for example, "Others suggest [that] training can be improved."
- Use plain language. For example, replace "aforementioned" with "previous" or "previously mentioned."
- Avoid the passive voice. Substitute pronouns (I, we, or they) and use active verbs; instead of "It is necessary to obtain," use "We need."

Double-Barreled Questions

A double-barreled question is a classic example of an unclear question. For example, the question, "Did you get skills training while in the program and a job after completing the program?" attempts to determine if there is a relationship between skills training and getting a job. But if the interviewee answers yes, this could mean yes to both parts, yes to the training part only, or yes to the job part only. Other interviewees, finding the question confusing, might not respond. They receive two questions but the opportunity to record only one answer. Both interviewee and interviewer may see the need for only one answer. Questions should be stated separately.

Double Negatives

Questions should avoid double negatives, which are difficult to answer. For example, "Indicate which of the organizational goals listed below are not considered unattainable within the two-year period" should be reworded to read, "Indicate which of the organizational goals listed below are considered attainable within the two-year period."

Extreme Words

It is best to avoid such words as all, none, everything, never, and others that represent extreme values. Rarely is a statement that uses such a word true, and the use of extreme words causes interviewees to avoid the end points of a scale. There are cases when the use of "all" or "none" is appropriate, but they are few. Where yes or no answers are expected, the results can be misleading. For example, if one employee is not covered in a question such as, "Are all of your employees covered by medical insurance?" a yes answer is impossible. A better question would be "About what percent of your employees are covered by medical insurance?" Alternatively, choices can be provided, as in Exhibit C-10.

Defining Terms

Where possible, key words and concepts used in questions should be defined. For example, a question about employees should define and clarify the term. Is it talking about part-time, full-time, permanent, temporary, volunteer, white-collar, or blue-collar? An example of how this might be done follows:

> Consider people who work for your company, are paid directly by your company, work at least 33 hours per week, and are viewed as permanent employees. What percent of these employees do this?

Of course, not all questions need to be preceded by such a definition. As earlier questions are developed, definitions evolve. One approach is to list

Exhibit C-10. Sample Question Avoiding Extreme Words by Offering Choices

What portion of your employees are covered by medical insurance? (READ THE CHOICES) *(Check one.)*
1. ☐ All or almost all 2. ☐ More than half but not all 3. ☐ About half 4. ☐ Some but less than half 5. ☐ None or hardly any

definitions in a separate section or on a card for interviewees to use as a reference.

BIAS WITHIN QUESTIONS

A question is biased when it causes interviewees to answer in a way that does not reflect their true positions on an issue. An interviewee may or may not be aware of the bias.

Problems result when the interviewees are

- unaware of the bias and influenced to respond the way the wording directs them.
- aware of the bias and deliberately answer in a way that does not reflect their opinions.
- refuse to answer because the question is biased.

Bias can appear in the statement portion of the question or in the response-alternative portion. Bias may also result when a question carries an implied answer, choices of answer are unequal, loaded words are used, or a scaled question is unbalanced.

Implied-Answer Bias

A question's wording can indicate the socially acceptable answer. An example is the question "Most of our employees have subscribed to the U.S. savings bond program. Have you subscribed?" Interviewees concerned about being different from the norm may answer yes even if they have not subscribed. The question could be restated as "Have you subscribed to the U.S. savings bond program?"

Questions can be worded to force some people to answer in certain directions. Yet the interviewees could be unaware of any bias in the wording. Such bias usually occurs when additional qualifying or identifying information is added to the question. There is bias in the question "Which plan is more acceptable to you: the one designed by Pat Brown, our chief economist, or the one designed by Chris Green, the consultant we hired?" An

Exhibit C-11. An Example of Unequal Choices

Whom do you feel is most responsible for the poor quality of the training program? *(Check all that apply.)*
1. ☐ Instructors 2. ☐ Counselors 3. ☐ High-paid managers who run the centers

Exhibit C-12. An Example of Equal Choices

Whom do you feel is most responsible for the poor quality of the training program? *(Check all that apply.)*
1. ☐ Instructors who teach the courses 2. ☐ Counselors who advise which courses to take 3. ☐ Managers who run the centers

interviewee who is not familiar with either plan may answer on the basis of whether the plan was generated internally or externally to the organization, though this may have little or nothing to do with the quality of the plan. A better presentation would be "Whose plan is more acceptable to you: Pat Brown's or Chris Green's?"

Bias Resulting from Unequal Choices

When response alternatives are created, it is important that they appear to be equal. If undue emphasis is given to one, it may be easier for the interviewee to select that one. Exhibit C-11 illustrates a question with unequal emphasis, and Exhibit C-12 corrects the unbalance. Alternative 3 in Exhibit C-11 is isolated from the two others because of the words "high-paid," which set those individuals apart from the others, and by the fact that alternative 3 is longer than the others.

Bias from Specific Words

When used in almost any context, certain words can be considered loaded, because they evoke strong feelings. American, freedom, equality, and justice generally evoke positive feelings, whereas communist, socialist, and bureaucrat may evoke negative feelings. Because it is difficult to control the emotional connotations of such words, it is usually best to avoid them.

Bias from Imbalance

In a scaled question it is important to avoid bias in the stem as well as in the response alternatives. A question that seeks to measure satisfaction with something should mention both ends of the scale equally. For example,

Exhibit C-13. A Question with Bias from Lack of Balance

How satisfied were you with the answers you received? *(Check one.)*
1. ☐ Extremely satisfied 2. ☐ Very satisfied 3. ☐ Neither satisfied nor dissatisfied 4. ☐ Generally dissatisfied 5. ☐ Very dissatisfied

Exhibit C-14. A Balanced Question

How satisfied or dissatisfied were you with the answers you received? *(Check one.)*
1. ☐ Extremely satisfied 2. ☐ Very satisfied 3. ☐ Neither satisfied nor dissatisfied 4. ☐ Generally dissatisfied 5. ☐ Very dissatisfied

Exhibit C-13 shows unbalance in both the stem and the alternatives, whereas Exhibit C-14 shows how this bias is eliminated.

CONSIDERATIONS FOR TELEPHONE INTERVIEWING INSTRUMENTS

In general, the same principles for developing interviews apply to the development of questions and answers for telephone surveys. However, some additional considerations come into play. The primary additional factor is that the cues available in face-to-face interviews are absent. It is not possible to observe the interviewee's reactions (including confusion, uncertainty, or hostility) and make allowable adjustments in conducting the interview. Making questions shorter, breaking multiple-choice questions into yes-no questions, and conducting some testing can overcome some of these difficulties.

Another loss in telephone interviewing arises from the impersonal nature of the telephone. An interviewer has a tendency to become flatter in presentation. The interviewer must counter this tendency by being continually aware of the enunciation of questions. In a questionnaire, some words are capitalized, underlined, or put into bold type to help the interviewer maintain appropriate pitch and emphasis.

THE PURPOSE OF PRETESTING

Pretesting and expert review constitute perhaps the least appreciated phase in the development of a structured interview. In the desire to meet deadlines for getting the job done, staff may ask, "Why not eliminate the pretest?" or "Do we need outside opinions on the interview form?" But these are perhaps the most important steps in developing an interview. It is an iterative process that uses continuing input from interviewers and technical specialists to derive the final product.

When the interviewer has little experience with a topic or when the interviewee has difficulty with a question, substantial work may be necessary to develop questions that will obtain the desired results. Research has shown that question formulation may alter results by as much as 50 percent. The pretest and expert review processes give the evaluators feedback as to whether the survey stands a chance of doing what it is designed to do.

In pretesting, the survey is tested with respondents drawn from the universe of people who will eventually be considered for the study interviews to predict how well the survey will work during actual data collection. The pretest seeks to determine whether

- the right questions are being asked to obtain the needed information.
- the contents or subject matter of each question is relevant to the respondent and the respondent has the knowledge to answer the question.
- the wording and procedures used in conducting the interviews are adequate to ensure that valid and reliable results are obtained.

Research has shown the following to be among the types of problems that arise with survey questions:

- Difficulties in asking the question because of complex sentence structure, tongue twisters, or words that are difficult to pronounce.
- Difficulties in comprehending the question because of difficult vocabulary, complex sentence structure, or lack of specificity about information or the form of information that is needed.
- Lack of common understanding of terms or concepts in the question because they are interpreted differently by different respondents or they are interpreted differently from what the interview designer intends.
- Difficulties in answering the question because the information is inaccessible or unavailable to the respondent to the extent that the respondent does not want to make the effort to obtain the answer.

PRETEST PROCEDURES

The number of pretests typically varies, depending on the size of the survey and the range of conditions that may affect the survey results. For structured interviewing of thousands of respondents, 25 to 75 pretests might be conducted. Sometimes, when the sample is less than 500, a dozen or fewer pretest cases are sufficient, provided they bracket the range of data collection conditions. The measurement specialist who designed the survey can suggest the correct number for a given survey. To a great degree, the pretest procedures for the structured interview simulate what would be done during actual data collection. It is important to test as many of the procedures involved in conducting a structured interview as possible, including the selection of and contact with the interviewees. In part, pretests should be conducted in the same mode to be used in the actual interviews — that is, the face-to-face interview pretested in person and telephone interviews tested over the telephone. However, telephone and mail surveys should also be tested partly in face-to-face interviews. For CATIs, which generally have fewer than 300 interviews, a dozen pretests might be sufficient. These tests should be conducted both in person and over the telephone.

Who Conducts the Pretest

Two types of staff should represent the organization in a pretest:

- The interviewer working on the job, because he or she can best address questions on the content of the survey and the background of the evaluation.
- The measurement specialist who designed the survey, because he or she needs to evaluate the interview process, including how the survey works, and suggest improvements.

The measurement specialist acts as the interviewer — that is, asks the questions on the first and perhaps the second pretest — while the interviewer observes. On subsequent tests, the interviewer asks the questions and the measurement specialist observers.

Selecting and Contacting Pretest Interviewees

Pretest interviewees are drawn (not necessarily randomly) from the universe being considered for the final study. If the universe is relatively homogeneous, the pretest subjects need not be exactly balanced as to various attributes. With a heterogeneous group, however, it is important to find a balanced group. Ideally, a survey is tested with several of each of the different kinds or types of individuals in a heterogeneous group.

Pretest interviewees should be contacted by telephone or in person to arrange a pretest session. If possible, procedures should be followed similar to those proposed for actual data collection. Interviewers should identify themselves, describe their organization and what it does, explain the nature of the study, and indicate the importance of their participation. If this is a face-to-face pretest, it is best to ask the interviewee to participate by arranging to meet in a place that is convenient to the interviewee and free of distractions. If this is a pretest of a telephone interview, a time should be arranged that is convenient for the interviewee.

Conducting the Pretest

The initial steps of a pretest are the same as for actual data collection. The interviewee should be given any appropriate background information, even if it was covered in the interview appointment. Because an interview is interactive, the interviewee will probably provide a great deal of feedback in addition to answering the questions. Problems with the survey or procedures often become evident immediately and may be dealt with then so that the interview can proceed. Often, if an interviewee does not understand an instruction, word, or concept, the interview cannot continue.

Ideally, however, it is desirable to run through the entire interview without getting sidetracked. This way, it is possible to examine the flow of the interview and estimate the total time needed to complete it.

During the pretest, the interviewer must do the following:

- Carry on the normal introduction and questioning of an interview without too much interruption in the flow.
- Provide explanations or try alternative wordings when the interviewee cannot or will not answer a question and note the changes introduced.
- Record the answers on the survey so the recording procedure and coding technique can be tested.
- Make notes on situations that occur during the interview that indicate problems with the instrument or procedures.
- Conduct a debriefing at the end of the interview to learn what the interviewee thought of the interview but did not express.

With respect to the second item, providing explanations or alternative wording must be done carefully because interviewer bias can occur. The interview is written as free of bias as possible. In deviating from the prescribed text, the interviewer may not have time to rephrase the question adequately and can make a slip in wording that favors or is slanted toward his or her approach to the situation.

For telephone interviews, it may be easier to conduct the pretests, and they may be more informative. The interviewee should be informed that a measurement specialist will be listening to refine the instrument. It may be possible to use a speaker phone to allow more members of the team to listen, take notes, and record answers without intruding. With the interviewee's permission, the interview may be taped to allow for more detailed examination of problems. With these possibilities, pretesting telephone interviews may be a lot smoother than pretesting face-to-face. However, some face-to-face interviews should be included.

Identifying Problems

After a pretest, the interviewer and the measurement specialist review the interview process and attempt to identify any problems that the interviewer has in asking the questions or the interviewees appear to have in answering the questions. If the pretests disclose problems such as ambiguous interpretation or other difficulties, the interview must be revised and tests must continue until the problems are resolved, even if this requires extra time. Premature termination of pretests can result in questionable data.

Major indicators of problems include the following:

- Slight changes by the interviewer in reading the question.
- Major changes by the interviewer in reading the question or not finishing reading the question.
- Interviewee interrupting the question reading with an answer.
- Difficulty in answering, as evidenced by the interviewee's nervousness; inconsistency in answers from question to question; inconsistency by reflecting back and changing answers; or taking too long to answer.
- Clarification, explanation, or repetition of the question requested by the interviewee.
- Qualified answer provided by the interviewee.
- Inadequate answer provided by the interviewee, including giving a different answer than one listed on the instrument or known to the interviewer.
- "Don't know" answer given by the interviewee.
- Refusal to answer by the interviewee.

The problems fall into two basic categories: those related to instrument design or administration and those concerning the interviewee's lack of knowledge or reluctance to answer. The first type can be controlled by the staff designing the instrument, whereas the second is merely recorded as observed behavior.

Pretest interviewers are not consistent in identifying problems with the questions or providing guidance for their revision. Responses can vary by as much as 50 percent when there are no adequate controls over the quality of the questions and procedures. Two techniques, categorization of respondent behavior and use of probe questions, are useful, particularly when the number of interviewers is large. The first method simply involves tabulating for each question how often each problem previously mentioned occurred across all interviews. A small percentage of interviews is expected to have some problem for each question. If, however, for a given question, a high percentage of interviews has a specific problem, this suggests that a question needs revision.

The second method, use of probe questions, can be used by itself or to clarify the nature of the problems identified from the first method. Special probe questions may be included in the interview or may be used at the end of an interview to ask interviewees to elaborate an answer, explain how they interpreted the questions or answers, or describe any difficulties. There are three types of probes:

- General probes ask for more information about particular questions or the entire interview.
- Information retrieval probes ask whether interviewees had a problem in recalling the information necessary to respond to the question.
- Comprehension probes ask interviewees how they interpreted particular questions or phrases.

PURPOSE OF EXPERT REVIEW

Because no survey is perfect, it is generally useful to seek outside commentary on an approach. Expert review on assignments using structured interviews can help determine the following:

- Whether the questions and the manner in which they are asked are adequate to answer the overall question posed in the evaluation.
- If the intended interviewee group has the knowledge to answer the questions.
- Whether the survey is constructed as well as possible within state-of-the-art confines.

In many instances, officials from the organization whose program is under review serve in this capacity. Obtaining input at this stage avoids potential problems after data collection, when time and money have already been spent. In other cases, staff in other design, methodology, and technical assistance groups, or individuals with subject-area or evaluation expertise can provide expert review. In particular, experts who belong to professional associations who provide lists of respondents can provide expert review.

Persons providing expert review do not act as interviewees. They do not answer the questions but instead provide a critique.

INSTRUMENT REDESIGN

The interviewer and the measurement specialist consider the results of the pretest and expert review and make appropriate changes to the survey. If changes are minor, the instrument can be used without further pretests; if they are extensive, another series of pretests may be necessary.

If pretesting can be spread over a longer period of time, more versions of the survey can be tested and fewer interviewees can be used with each version. Changes that are obviously needed can be made, and the revised version can be used in the next pretest. This allows use of a relatively more perfect version on each round of pretests.

In most cases, an organization's interviewers conduct structured interviews for studies, but occasionally a company uses employees of other agencies or contractors. Regardless, the interviewers must be trained in the purpose of the evaluation and the procedures for conducting the interview.

TRAINING METHODS

Each organization has various ways to train interviewers and help them maintain their skills throughout the data-collection period: a job kick-off conference, an interview booklet, role-playing and field practice, and supervisory field visits and telephone contacts.

Kick-off Conference

For most projects of any size, a division holds a kick-off conference to tell the staff from the regions and other divisions the purpose of the evaluation, to make assignments, and to answer questions. When a project is to include structured interviewing in the data-collection phase, the conference is usually extended so the interviewers can be given detailed instructions on the use of the survey. Preferably, all potential interviewers should attend.

If a region sends only one representative to the kick-off conference, for example, he or she should be an individual who will be conducting interviews for the study. Not all aspects of the training can be written into the interview booklet (discussed in the next section), thus practice sessions must involve, along with the measurement specialist, those who will actually conduct interviews and possibly train others in the region to do so.

The training begins with the project manager and the measurement specialist reviewing the purpose of the study and how the interview data will fit into its overall objectives. Then the data collection procedures are covered in detail, using the interview booklet. The trainers discuss the interview form, question by question, including the need for the data, possible rephrasing to be used if a question is not understood by the interviewee, how to record the answers, and other matters they think could arise. The trainees can ask questions, clarify items, catch typographical errors in the survey, and suggest possible changes from their experience. Even at such a late date as the kick-off conference, changes can be made in the survey to preclude problems being carried into the actual interviews.

Potential problems the trainers usually make special efforts to address include making sure that the interviewers do the following:

- *Know what an adequate answer to each question is.* Without this knowledge, they may accept an inadequate answer. A structured interview is set up to show the interviewer, by means of the response choices, what is adequate and what is inadequate. For this to be learned, the interviewer must understand the survey.
- *Ask the questions correctly.* The words are there on paper; the interviewers need to be persuaded to use them in the way they are presented to ensure standardization of meaning and delivery and elimination of bias. Even though the survey is pretested, some interviewees will still have trouble understanding the language. The interviewer must know enough about the question that if the interviewer has to reword the question, the rewording will not violate the intent of the question.
- *Do not omit questions they think are answered by other questions.* Answers are expected to all questions unless instructions call for an item to be skipped or the interviewee refuses to answer. (Refusal can be considered an answer.) If the interviewee gives the answer to a question before it is asked, the interviewer should either ask the question anyway or give it as a statement for the interviewee to affirm.
- *Do not introduce bias in the way they ask the questions.* This is always important.

Interview Booklet

When there are few interview questions and they are not very complex or difficult and the staff members who will conduct the interviews helped develop the survey, the kick-off conference alone can be used to inform the interviewers in detail how each question should be handled.

If a large-scale interview effort is undertaken, project staff may prepare a booklet that discusses in detail each question in the DCI. Typically, booklets cover not only the interview questions but also matters such as sampling procedures, contacts with interviewees, and coding procedures. These are discussed in the following sections.

Sampling Procedures. When statistical sampling procedures are to be used to select interviewees, the booklet shows the interviewer how to identify the universe and select the sample. The booklet may include a random-number table, when necessary, and describe both simple random samples and more complex two-stage procedures.

Interviewee-Contact Procedures. Rules are provided for contacting the potential interviewee and deciding what to do if the person refuses or cannot be located. An example is given of a phone conversation to set up the interview. Also covered is the log interviewers must keep of all interview contacts to ensure that proper sampling is maintained. The log makes it possible to adjust the universe later and examine possible effects of non-response. For CATIs, a computer handles many of the contact and logging procedures automatically. How this is to be accomplished should be described to the interviewers during training.

Coding Procedures. The booklet shows interviewers how to code the various types of question to facilitate editing and keypunching the answers and reviews different types of questions. This is handled automatically for CATIs.

Role-Playing Practice

This is nothing more than two staff members taking turns playing interviewer and interviewee, a training method that should start at the kick-off conference as a group session with the measurement specialist observing and critiquing. The role-playing can continue when the staff members return to their regions, particularly if regional staff members who did not attend the conference will also be conducting interviews.

Such role-playing gives staff members the chance to become familiar with the instrument from both sides of the interview. The person playing the interviewee should challenge the interviewer by giving him a hard time, perhaps refusing to answer questions or pretending not to understand them. Sometimes this serves to show the weaknesses of questions that are unclear or lack sufficient response alternatives. If so, the project manager or measurement specialist should be notified so that the items can be changed or clarification can be given to all interviewers.

For CATIs, the interviewers must also be trained in the software requirements. This should be done after being trained in the details of a paper version of the survey. The computer training first focuses on the mechanics of using the computer for a CATI, showing the interviewers how to start the CATI, move the cursor and step through each screen, move back and forth between questions, and identify particular situations that may arise.

After the essentials of the survey and the computer have been covered, the interviewers can proceed to role-playing, this time using the computer setup for office-to-office mock interviews. The project manager or measurement specialist should observe these sessions to identify not only weaknesses in the survey but also any difficulties in using the computer. This role-playing should be practiced for a half to a full day.

Field Practice

Once interviewers are in the field at the first site, they should oversample the number of interviewees needed for that site and use some for field-practice interviews. These interviews are planned as throw-away cases and identified as such in advance of the interview. The data derived from an interview are not used in the final analysis, regardless of whether the interview went well or poorly. Interviewing real interviewees who do not count gives interviewers a chance to get rid of any anxiety and test their approach. The interviewees, however, should not be told that it is a practice session. To them, this is the real thing; they will, therefore, exhibit all the cautions and concerns of any interviewee.

Obviously, field practice takes some time and should be built into the project schedule. After practice, the interviewers should discuss any problems they had and decide where they need to change their approach or learn more. Any lasting concerns should be relayed to the project manager or the measurement specialist.

Supervisory Field Visits

Normally, the project manager makes field visits during the course of an evaluation. A visit early in the data-collection phase, when interviewing has just begun, is valuable. It allows the project manager to review the procedures being used to conduct the interviews and observe some interviews firsthand. This quality-assurance checking enables the project manager to ascertain that interviewers are carrying out the standard practices designed into the structured interview procedures. If possible, the measurement specialist should participate in some of the visits.

In some instances, it may be useful to tape initial interviews, with the interviewee's permission, to remove any final problems associated with the interview administration.

The project manager and measurement specialist form a team that keeps interviewers informed of changes in procedure and receives comments from the field on progress and problems encountered. These telephone contacts serve as the final step in training interviewers.

INTERVIEWER QUALIFICATIONS

Many interviews are highly sensitive, and the data to be obtained can be influenced by subtle elements that the interviewer controls. When an organization uses outside sources to supply interviewers, it usually retains the right to examine the work of interviewers and, if there is cause, suggest that some be replaced. The same applies to interviewers to whom the region or division assigns the project. Staff members who are reluctant to conduct the necessary interviews or exhibit some bias may not be right for the job and could jeopardize the data-collection effort.

For CATIs, interviewers' skill level and content knowledge can be lower than for face-to-face interviews because the questions are generally simpler and fewer probes need to be used. As a result, contracts for CATIs or the use of short-term, part-time staff have been quite successful and provide alternatives to the use of evaluators.

Supervisors should evaluate the qualifications that interviewers exhibit during the various training opportunities. If there are any problems that cannot be corrected through retraining, these interviewers should be replaced.

SELECTION OF INTERVIEWEES

For some structured interviews, because there is only one person who fits the category of interviewee, no selection process is needed. When complex sampling techniques are used and a list of interviewees is generated by computer, control over the selection and contact of interviewees can be automated, as the following sections describe.

CONTACTING POTENTIAL INTERVIEWEES

Once the potential interviewees have been selected, someone must contact them, explain what the organization is doing and why it needs their assistance, and arrange an appointment. The interview booklet sets out rules to be followed in contacting the interviewees.

Frequently, when structured interviews are used, the universe list is developed for a given point in time and a sample is drawn. By the time the sample is contacted for interviews, months may have passed. This means some of the people selected for initial telephone contact will have moved away or otherwise become inaccessible to interviewers. Thus, it is wise to oversample and set up rules for replacing individuals who cannot be located.

When contacting interviewees by phone, interviewers should use a standardized approach. This ensures that they do not omit any important information. Naturally, if unexpected events occur, it may be necessary to deviate from this guide. The interview booklet may contain some samples of unexpected events and provide some guidance on how to deal with them.

Interviewers should maintain a log of all attempted contacts, with a record of each interviewee's name and address, telephone number, date and time of the attempted contact, and the result. This information will be of use later in determining the possible effects of nonrespondents on the results. It also gives the analyst a means of adjusting the universe and plays a role when response-weighing is used.

For CATIs, a database of respondents can easily be generated and used to provide automated call sheets. Certain information, such as the time when an interview was conducted, can be entered automatically by the computer. In addition, if information about the interviewee is already available from other sources, it can be entered directly into the record being generated without having to ask the interviewee (unless some verification is wanted). Finally, when the interview is completed, selected information can be transferred to the automated call sheets to record the progress in administering the survey.

INTERVIEW ARRANGEMENTS

When an individual is interviewed for an evaluation or audit, the interviewee usually is doing the organization a favor. The interview arrangements, including time and site, should therefore be as convenient as possible for the interviewee.

This may mean conducting the interview at an hour that is inconvenient for the interviewer, such as early morning or late evening. The location might be the interviewer's office, an audit site, space provided by the organization under review, or some other public place.

If the interview contains sensitive questions, holding the interview in certain locations might create difficulties. Such a setting might cause interviewees to omit negative comments out of fear that this information would be overheard.

For CATIs, the same general principles are used to set up an interview. The interviewer should assume that his or her first contact with the interviewee will not be a satisfactory time to conduct the interview and ask the interviewee when would be a good time to set aside a specific amount of time. The interviewer should be particularly alert to any impatience on the part of the interviewee in arranging the time. One method is to mail a postcard to the interviewee asking for a convenient time. Sometimes it is useful to highlight the main topics the interview will cover. In addition, if there is specific information that the interviewee will need to gather before the interview, this should be included on the postcard or in a letter.

If the interview is to be taped or if a supervisor is listening, the interviewee must be so informed and their consent obtained. If the interviewee objects, alternative arrangements should be available. Acceptable alternatives should be described in the interview guide.

PROTECTING THE INTERVIEWEE

Some interview situations result in the interviewees' speaking of themselves or others negatively. This could come from asking questions on such sensitive issues as personal habits or behavior, attitudes (for example, political or religious views), or reactions to an employer, boss, or employees. To obtain cooperation from interviewees and improve the quality of the data and the response rate, the interviewer may need to grant some kind of assurance to the interviewees that the data collected will not be used in a manner that could harm them.

When first contacting interviewees and again when meeting for the interview, the interviewer should give them some idea of what types of question you wish to ask and seek their cooperation. This is called obtaining informed consent: revealing the contents of the interview in advance of the actual questioning, thus giving the interviewee a chance to refuse to comply with the interview request. Some organizations use a more defined procedure in which the interviewee is asked to sign a statement of understanding. Providing advance information is preliminary to actual guarantee of protection, which takes the form of confidentiality or anonymity.

When an interviewer evaluator could associate the interviewee's name with specific responses but promises not to do so, the interviewer has promised to preserve the interview's confidentiality. They must obtain specific written approval before making pledges of confidentiality.

An interview is anonymous if the staff performing the work on the evaluation is unaware of the responses of individual interviewees. When data is collected through face-to-face interviews conducted by interviewers, granting anonymity to the interviewees is impossible.

CONDUCTING INTERVIEWS

Each participant in the interview — interviewer and interviewee — has a role to perform and a set of behaviors that assist in the performance. Because the role and behaviors of each influence the conduct of the interview, they affect the other participant. The interviewer's role and behaviors can be prescribed and acquired through training, whereas the interviewee's role and behaviors must be observed by the interviewer, who seeks to modify them as necessary to successfully complete the interview.

DEVELOPING RAPPORT AND SHOWING INTEREST

The interviewer must seek to establish a balanced relationship with the interviewee and to appear as an empathetic, friendly individual who is not too different from the interviewee but who is also an independent, unbiased, and honest collector of data. The interviewer's appearance, verbal mannerisms, body language, and voice determine the rapport, starting with the contact that sets up the interview.

Interviewers must make their verbal and voice cues calm and unflustered. They must speak so the interviewee does not have to strain to hear and understand. Changes in voice inflection, sighs, or other noises give clues to feelings or moods, as do facial expressions and body language. They must be controlled so that the interviewee does not pick up impatience, disapproval, or other negative feelings. Likewise, the interviewer should control expressions of positive feelings or agreement with what the interviewee says.

It is important that the interviewer be aware of characteristic nonlinguistic cues such as change in voice, facial expressions, or gestures because as much as half of the communication that takes place during the interview is conveyed by these modes of expression. Failure to understand these cues may result in miscommunication.

Appearance is still another variable that influences rapport and, therefore, the tone of the interview. Interviewers should dress to fit both the interview and the interviewee.

GIVING THE INTERVIEWEE A REASON TO PARTICIPATE

Generally, interviewees do not benefit directly from the information that they give to an organization. Why, then, should they agree to give their time for an interview? The reasons are various. Some interviewees are obliged to cooperate with interviewers because of their positions and to provide information on how money is being spent. Such individuals usually understand why they should participate and need only be told something about the evaluation procedures. In other cases, greater explanation may be required.

Interviewees who are not aware of the importance of the evaluation and how they can help may not give sincere and well-thought-out answers. Explanations to them, therefore, are important to the validity of the resulting data.

ASKING QUESTIONS IN A PRESCRIBED ORDER AND MANNER

The order in which the questions appear in the structured interview is not accidental. Questions are ordered so as to lead the interviewee through various topics, correctly position sensitive questions, and hold the interviewee's interest. To the greatest extent possible, the interviewer must maintain this order. The words and phrasing used in the questions also have been carefully chosen and tested. For the sake of standardization and understandability, it is important that these be used as planned.

ENSURING UNDERSTANDING

At times, an interviewee will not understand a question and will indicate this by telling the interviewer so, not answering, or providing an answer that seems inconsistent or wrong. When this happens, the interviewer should use an appropriate probing technique such as the following:

- Repeat the question.
- Give an expectant pause.
- Repeat the respondent's reply.
- Make neutral questions or comments, such as "Anything else?" "Any other reason?" "Any others?" "How do you mean?" "Could you tell me more about your thinking on that?" "Would you tell me what you have in mind?" "What do you mean?" "Why do you feel that way?" "Which would be closer to the way you feel?"

To maintain the meaning of the questions and not to bias them, interviewers should do this probing with care. These kinds of probes should be worked out during the pretest. Rephrasing the question or adding new questions should be avoided. If all probes have been tried and rephrasing or adding questions is the only alternative, notes to that effect should be added next to the responses.

PREVENTING BIAS

Bias can be expressed in the way interviewers pose a query, in the introduction of their own ideas into a probe, or in adding certain verbal emphasis or using certain body language. All these can destroy the neutrality that should characterize the presentation. When listening to the interviewee's answer, interviewers can also filter out portions of the message that alter the true response.

OBTAINING SUFFICIENT ANSWERS

The interviewer must judge when an answer is sufficient before going to the next question. If the answer is incomplete or vague, he or she should ensure that the question is understood or draw more out of the interviewee to complete the answer. At times, the interviewee is allowed to answer questions in an open-ended fashion, while the interviewer matches each answer to one of a set of responses on the interview form. He or she must be sure that the interviewee has sufficient information to select one of the answers. Sometimes, the interviewer must select two or more responses (not just one) from the set and ask the interviewee which one best matches his or her answer. This should be done, however, only as a last resort and only after giving the respondent ample time to respond.

On other occasions, an interviewee may not have the answer in mind but may need to refer to documents or ask someone else. If this can be done conveniently and within a short time, the interviewee should be encouraged to do so.

The interviewer can also check the accuracy of the answers by asking for supporting information from the interviewee. Sometimes the design of the instrument has built into it questions to which answers have already been obtained from files or from other people in advance. These questions can be used to check the accuracy with which the interviewee is answering. Under-reporting of information is often found. As the length of time since a subject event increases, there is a greater tendency for the interviewee either to forget the event occurred or to recall only parts of it.

SHOWING SENSITIVITY TO INTERVIEWEE BURDEN

Before conducting an interview, the interviewer should give the interviewee a general statement of how long it is expected to take. The interviewer is then under some obligation to adhere to this time limitation.

Frequently, interviewees prolong their answers by adding examples, critical incidents, or other stories. If no one has a time problem, this extension of the interview is acceptable. If time is critical, however, the interviewer should speed up the interview so as not to lose valuable answers at the end. Besides the length of time taken, the interview can be burdensome because of the amount of work the interviewee needs to go through to produce the information requested. If a relatively unimportant question requires a significant amount of time or energy by the interviewee, it may not be worth pursuing.

Analyzing Reasons for Nonparticipation

When trying to contact individuals to set up interviews, the interviewer can talk to them or someone who has information about them.

If they cannot or refuse to be interviewed, the interviewer can try to discover why. Then, the interviewer can attempt to determine whether the reasons given for nonparticipation relate to critical questions in the interview.

Interviewing a Subsample on Critical Questions

A second approach to the nonrespondent problem is to select a subsample of those not available for an interview (or the entire group, if it is small enough) and conduct a short phone survey of them, using some of the critical questions on the instrument. Of course, this does not help if the people could not be located in the first place. If most, however, were found but at first refused an interview because of time considerations, it may be possible to collect data on some questions on the phone. The answers are then compared to those collected in the normal interviewing process, using statistical procedures to test for significant differences. Questions on which the two groups differ significantly might then be eliminated from the final analysis.

Comparing Demographic Information

Many times, there is a rich database on a collection of demographic variables for all potential interviewees. Thus if it is not possible to obtain partial interview information from a subsample, it is possible to compare the demographic variables for those interviewed and those not. Significant differences on a certain proportion of critical demographic variables would cast doubt that the two groups were essentially the same and indicate that the absence of these individuals could alter the overall results.

Assuming the Worst Case

Some of the questions posed will have yes-no answers. In this case, someone must determine whether those who did not respond could have reversed the consensus of those who did.

NONRESPONDENT PROBLEM

Rarely can an entire sample be interviewed because of deaths, inability to locate people, refusals to be interviewed, and so on. For telephone interviews, the nonrespondent problem is usually significantly less. They frequently have high response rates.

To combat the nonrespondent problem, organizations usually randomly sample a greater number of people than is statistically required. Nonrespondents can be replaced by randomly drawn substitutes.

Usually, making a small number of substitutions has no effect on analysis of the final data. When a larger number of substitutions is made, for example 20 percent or more, concern may surface that the people you were unable to interview represent a unique portion of the universe. If queried, this portion might have given dramatically different answers to all or some of the questions and altered the final results of the data collection.

There are several ways to make sure that the data would not have changed much had these individuals been contacted. They are discussed in the following sections.

Some questions require collecting additional information. Nothing short of obtaining the interviewees' answers to the questions is satisfactory in this case.

DATA ANALYSIS

The analysis to be done is determined to a great degree by the project objectives that have been established for the structured interview.

First-Level Analysis

First-level analysis concentrates on a description of the data — for example, how many responded to each response alternative, both in absolute numbers and on a percentage basis. For example, a question may have asked, "Did you complete high school?" A description of the data would show how many and what percentage responded "yes" and how many said "no."

In the language of analysis, this type of description of the data is commonly referred to as frequency tabulations or frequency tables. Although not the only analytic activity under this first-level analysis, it is normally the most significant activity.

Often, a computer run is made to obtain frequency tabulations during the data-verification phase because it will show all values keypunched for every question. A review of the run will disclose possible errors in the database. In the previous example, yes answers may be coded as "1" and no answers as "2." Any other number showing up for this question would stem from an error on the part of the interviewer or the keypuncher.

Second-Level Analysis

Second-level analysis begins where the description of the data stops. In this next level of analysis, perhaps the most useful to most organizations' efforts, data is analyzed one question at a time. Certain statistics, such as the mean and median, can be obtained with the description of the data for questions where such statistics would be useful or appropriate. If a sample other than a simple random sample has been used, the number and percentages shown on the frequency tabulations' run must be weighted before projections are made. Therefore, it would be wise to consult a sampling statistician before using the numbers in a briefing or report.

The next step is to test the associations between pairs of questions in response to hypotheses established during the design phase. If the data shows one, could it stem from the fact that a sample was studied and not the entire population? Such statistical measures as chi-square analysis and correlation analysis are often used to determine how certain researchers can be that apparent associations between responses to two questions do not stem from chance. On many assignments, second-level analysis is as far as the analysis of questionnaire or interview data goes.

Third-Level Analyses

Third-level analyses are more complex than the other levels of analysis. They normally take into account many variables at one time and address more complex questions. Third-level analyses often address differences between subgroups of surveyed cases — what factors differentiate students who repay federal loans in a timely manner from those who do not — or investigate the influence that a set of factors may have on a single variable — what factors influence the amount of loans made by the Small Business Administration.

Two of the many analytic tools available to investigate these more complex analytic questions are multiple regression analysis and discriminant function analysis.

The nature and complexity of the analysis phase of a project can vary dramatically, depending primarily on the objective established for the project. The analysis that addresses cause-and-effect questions is much more difficult than the analysis for descriptive or normative questions. Regardless of the type of question being addressed, several statistical tools are available for the analysis phase of the evaluation. Selecting the most appropriate is not easy. Evaluators and auditors should obtain assistance from a specialist for this phase.

ANALYSIS OF OPEN-ENDED QUESTIONS

Answers to open-ended questions may range from a few words to several sentences. Interviewees typically give the interviewer some salient ideas that come quickly to mind but leave out some important factors. Open-ended questions do not help interviewees consider an identical range of factors. After conducting several interviews, interviewers may supplement the question by asking the interviewee about factors not mentioned, but such supplemental questions will not be standard among interviewers. Thus, the interviewees as a group are not responding to identical questions.

The proper analysis of open-ended questions requires the use of a complicated, time-consuming process called content analysis. In brief, the researcher must read and reread several of the written responses, come up with some scheme to categorize the answers (in essence, develop a set of alternative responses), and develop rules for assigning responses to the categories. Even with a set of rules, people can categorize answers differently. Therefore, three or four people must go through each completed interview and categorize the answers. A majority of them must agree to ensure a reliable database.

Because content analysis is time-consuming, the answers to open-ended questions are often left unanalyzed. The evaluator or auditor in reporting may quote from one or a few selected responses, but open-ended interviews generally do not produce uniform data that can be compared, summed, or further analyzed to answer the evaluation or audit questions.

Index